Past Life Regression

Past Life Regression

A Manual for Hypnotherapists to
Conducted Effective Past Life Regression Sessions

Kemila Zsange, RCCH

Journey Beyond Production

First Paperback Edition 2015

Journey Beyond Production

ISBN 9781511601399

To Devin Xingyao Yu ~

my beautiful nephew with whom I conducted my very first
effective Past Life Regression session, in this lifetime

Table of Content

Chapter 6

During a Past Life Regression   99

Chapter 7
After Death 133

Chapter 8
Post Regression Contextualization and Exit 149

Chapter 9
Afterward 153

Introduction

This book is the result of preparing for the first annual conference of the Association of Registered Clinical Hypnotherapists (ARCH Canada), where I gave a presentation of the same title.

In one of my earlier classes when I was a student of hypnotherapy, one day the instructor said, "You should never do Past Life Regression on purpose. If it spontaneously happens, deal with it." I remember sitting there, thinking, "If I'm not to do Past Life Regression on purpose, then why on earth am I sitting here?"

It was that inner knowing that got me onto this journey. Although, based on the attitude from my hypnotherapy instructor, one could easily imagine that I was not "properly trained" as a Past Life regressionist, that inner knowing has been the driving engine for me on this journey. As with many other things in my life, including the English language, to a large degree, I am a self-taught Past Life regressionist. Every single person I have worked with has been my best teacher.

However, even when I just started, when a person asked me, "How long have you been doing Past Life Regression?" I'd always answer it jokingly, "For about five hundred years." Together we'd have a good laugh.

Yet inside me this answer feels just right. I've had knowledge of myself, since childhood, that seems far beyond what living this lifetime can explain, including awareness of different roles, genders, eras. Doing Past Life Regression excites me. It enables me to help others see a depth and height to themselves, rather than that linear limited and judgment-based perspective that people have come to learn as "me".

A large part of this book is a manual for conducting effective Past Life Regression sessions in a step-by-step manner. This book is full of scripts. You do not need to go through all the scripts in one session. But the scripts are there when you feel that you do need them in any particular situation. And, as with any script, all of those in this book are meant to be adapted to the individuals and circumstances you are working with.

A good Past Life regressionist, as a good hypnotherapist, for that matter, is beyond any script; but like learning a language, unless we are born a native speaker of a language, the quickest way to learn a language is through grammar and with immersion. In practicing the excellence in being a Past Life regressionist, this book is like that grammar book, with practice, practice, and practice, eventually you will not need this book at all.

Throughout this book, I use the term "subconscious mind" and "unconscious mind" interchangeably. I mostly prefer using "unconscious mind" but in some cases the term "subconscious mind" may fit better. Within scripts, I use ellipses to indicate a pause when speaking.

I had wished to have such a book as a stepping-stone when I first started. And I have developed the materials, tested them, used them, and improved them throughout the years for myself. Now I present this book for other Past Life regressionists who may feel the same calling.

Kemila Zsange

April, 2015
Vancouver, BC Canada

CHAPTER 1

When and When Not to Do Past Life Regression Sessions?

The first rule of thumb I use is: Do Past Life Regression when asked to. It's as simple as that. People ask for it for all sorts of reasons – spiritual growth, getting in touch with the depth of themselves, curiosity, physical symptoms or emotional problems, irrational fears and phobias, understanding relationships or talents, life purpose, etc.

Sometimes, though, a person may present a problem, and self-diagnose that the problem originated in a past life. Be cautious in this case. You can tell them that the problem may or may not have originated from a past life, but that together you can find out. Give them the option of starting by exploring a past life, which may possibly be the cause of their problem; or by focusing directly on the cause of their problem, which may also lead to a past life. Be clear with the person that their choice may influence what they get from the session. This way, client and therapist can make an informed decision together.

You can suggest exploring past lives as a solution to problems when you have the sense that someone is open to that avenue and you have already explored other alternatives. I get the sense of a person's religious or spiritual beliefs from my Client Intake Form where there is one line asking for "Religion". A lot of people who I have worked with put "spiritual" on that line, or they simply leave it blank. At their first appointment, I'll briefly talk with them about their spiritual/religious outlook, to get a sense if they are open to Past Life Regression or not.

This sense of their beliefs can also help me guide them when spontaneous past life recall occurs. When a client in trance receives spontaneous information about a past life or reincarnation, it could be confusing for them if it does not fit with their existing belief system. We can use specific language to address these clients, resolve charged energy, and release trauma, by using the language of "imagination", rather than calling it a past life.

One day, a middle-aged woman I'll call Sally came to see me. She worked in a casino as a dealer. She felt stuck. She had a sense that there was more that she could do and be, but she didn't know what it was. In order to have a sense of clarity and direction to move forward, she decided to have a hypnotherapy session.

Sally acknowledged that she had always had a wonderful imagination. "Inside my mind I am still childlike," said Sally, and she seemed to like it that way.

Her "childlike" mind took us spontaneously to the 19th century, in Mississippi, where a woman named Mary was a published author. There was an initial confusion as Sally felt that she was the woman. For the whole session, I encouraged her to "continue to imagine this, and see where your imagination in hypnosis can take us. In this imagination, you can speak as if you *are* Mary. The imagination from your unconscious mind will eventually give us a key to unlock your purpose and talent, so that we can gain clarity and the direction moving forward as Sally."

Thus we had a full past life recall in the name of imagination. Only after the session, as Sally was trying to rationalize what she experienced, did I mention briefly that she may have had what other people call a Past Life Experience, although it didn't matter what she called it. I told her that she could do some research and conclude on her own. Meanwhile she could take this as a symbol from her own unconscious mind, because her unconscious mind did have a strong sense of direction and clarity for her.

The experience felt real and made sense to Sally, as she always felt there was a book or two within her, waiting to be written. It was her mind that didn't believe she could write even though writing had always made her feel good. After that one session, Sally understood that a gift was presented to her from her unconscious mind. And she said she was going to start writing, even if only a journal to start with. I asked her to keep in touch, as I'd like to be the first person to buy her book when one is published.

Thus there are three main reasons to conduct Past Life Regressions: when a client asks for it; when it may be helpful and a client is open for it; and when it spontaneously happens. It is not advised to conduct Past Life Regressions in other circumstances. For the purpose of this book, we will focus on the first case – when a client asks for a Past Life Regression, and we do it on purpose.

Does a person need to believe in reincarnation to have a successful Past Life Regression? No. A Past Life Regression is an experience. What we believe is secondary to our experience. We do not need to believe in anything to have a certain experience of something.

Not only my clients, but I also don't know if I "believe" in reincarnation. For me, reincarnation is just a word, an idea, a concept, a label; the definition of it may not fully describe the true reality. We as hypnotherapists can learn to facilitate certain experiences without buying into any particular beliefs.

I feel that answering the question "do you believe in reincarnation?" is like answering the question "do you believe in sunsets?"

On one hand, they both seem quite obvious to me. I have facilitated hundreds of Past Life Regressions; and have seen many sunsets. On the other hand, we know that the sun never rises or sets for the Earth. The illusion (and the beauty) of a sunset is real regardless of the fact that the Earth is rotating on its axis rather than the sun rotating around the Earth. Reincarnation is not technically a correct term as time does not exist - Everything is here and now, but it is real for the experience, just like the sunset.

Reasons for PLR
client helps
helpful
spirit anxiously happen

CHAPTER 2

Intake

Client intake is when we gather information from the client, set the stage for the session, and answer any up front questions the client may have. You want to gather as much relevant information as you can, and also gain a sense of where a client's spiritual awareness is at.

Intake is the time when you can write down notes and form some purposeful questions for the hypnosis part of the session. Covering a whole life (and sometimes more than one lifetime) in a single regression session means that you have to be like a detective, and to have a focus, so that you know what kinds of questions to ask in order to guide your clients. During the session, it is our job as therapists to respect the mental patterns and emotional problems of our clients, while helping them find relevance to their presenting problems, and promoting their healing. Taking some notes during intake will also help you contextualize at the end of the session.

My client Tina came to see me for fear of public speaking. And she wanted to experience a past life. Tina's subconscious mind took us to a life where she lived as a young girl in India. She married a man she loved. He was from an upper caste. Even though they loved each other very much, living in his family, she had to endure the hostility of his mother and sisters. They treated her badly while he was not home. They hated it when she gave "new ideas" to him. Eventually they found reasons to stone her one dark night. The young girl died thinking, "I did nothing wrong, but causing attention to myself can lead to my death." And she felt powerlessness.

During the contextualization I pointed out the family didn't stone the girl because she was powerless. On the contrary, they did it because they were afraid of her. They were afraid because they perceived power in her. They wouldn't care to kill a powerless person. But they wanted to make sure they kill their threat. "They saw you as a threat because they perceived you as one with power. You may not choose to embrace it, but you have it. Now in a peaceful country, you can choose what to do with that power that you have."

With that context in place, Tina realized a connection between the issue she presented with and her past life experience, and she felt self-empowered upon leaving.

Some people may have a certain agenda, such as "I want to see my connection to the Druids in 17th century Ireland". When this type of situation happens, it helps to clarify with the client that sometimes it's not up to the conscious mind to set the agenda, just as it is not up to the therapist to set the agenda. Let them know that their unconscious mind may have another agenda. It may want to review the life of interest to their conscious mind, or their unconscious mind may want to review another life first. Let them know that whatever life comes up and presents itself, it is because that life needs to come up at this time. My experience is that it is always better to encourage a client to follow their unconscious agenda because it allows them to learn and trust their unconscious mind.

After they've given their background, it is useful to ask about their understanding of hypnosis, hypnotherapy, and whether they have had previous experience or not. If they have, ask whether it was a positive one or not. The answers to these questions can guide you in the manner in which you conduct the session.

Setting the stage for the session provides clients with a framework for the session, and helps them relax and set aside their analytical judgment. Begin by letting them know that past life recall is not about having a good memory. It actually has nothing to do with memory as our ordinary sense of memory is. Past Life Regression is done through re-experiencing or re-living the moment, instead of remembering.

Analogies are very helpful in preparing clients for regression. Explain that what they are doing is like playing with jigsaw puzzles. During the regression is like the time for organizing the pieces. Only when all of the pieces have been turned over can they be put together and made into a picture. Similarly, people can't do a good job collecting the data and analyzing the data at the same time. It's like an athlete can't perform and think about how he's doing at the same time. Assure clients that it's not their job to make sense of what comes up in the moment when it comes up. Their job is to focus internally and relax, and to just say directly whatever comes up in their awareness. Clarify that you will help them make sense of it at the end of the session. That helps take some of the burden away from them.

I use a different analogy to describe the deepening process and entering into trance. I'd describe our daily life is like a surface of a lake. We move from one place to another, with continuous thoughts of "what's next", "what's next". This creates a lot of motion on the surface of the lake, with a lot of waves or ripples. For many people, that's all that they know about their lives. It's very linear. From a hypnosis perspective, it's the normal beta brainwave.

But as with any lake, there is always a depth. People may not be aware of it, as they are caught up in the busyness of life, the activities on the surface of the lake. The way to see what's underneath is not by trying hard, or harder. Trying hard creates more waves and ripples. When we stop trying, such as when we go into hypnosis, we relax the body, and the mind becomes passive. This lack of activity creates a natural stillness on the surface of the lake. Then the lake becomes clear, and the bottom of the lake can be easily discerned. And since the clients have chosen to come to see

14

you for a Past Life Regression experience, they are ready to explore another dimension of the lake.

To describe to a client about setting aside their conscious analytical mind, I'd talk to them about how, during our daily activities, our conscious mind is the driver of the vehicle of their life. It thinks, analyses, rationalizes and figures things out. It works hard, but they are not here in my office to work with their conscious mind because they already know how to do that. A hypnotic trance is like having the conscious mind take the passenger seat, so that their unconscious mind, the mind that has the answers, recourses, memories and solutions, can come out and drive the vehicle. My role, as a hypnotherapist, is like a tourist guide. I know the territory, and they know where they want to go. Together we go there.

Having driven the vehicle for so long, the new passenger may doubt the new driver's ability. Since the experiences coming up from the unconscious mind bypass the conscious mind, their conscious mind may have critical thoughts, such as, "I must be making this up, because it doesn't make sense." Reiterate that the key is not to be engaged with their thoughts, either negatively or positively. A good driver always focuses on the road. They should acknowledge what they hear from the "passenger", and return back to their focus again and again. This suggestion will be reinforced during the hypnosis induction.

The stories and analogies that I have described above are simply ones that I have found to be effective for explaining the process to clients. Feel free to experiment and develop your own unique voice for connecting with your own Past Life Regression clients.

Two Commonly Asked Questions

Intake is also the time to address two of the most commonly asked questions. The first we have previously mentioned – **"What if I made everything up?"** Despite being very emotional, such as crying or sobbing while going through the Past Life Regression process, people can still think afterwards that they have made everything up. In doing this, they completely cut themselves off from the inner flow of their own vitality, the intelligence within.

If the question is presented before or during a Past Life Regression, focus on encouraging them to be engaged in the process only:

Most people can directly answer my questions but the conscious mind can tell them that they make it up. I want to let you know that's okay. Don't engage the conscious mind. Set it aside and go for what comes up even though you may think you make it up.

Your task, should you choose to accept it, is to not do anything other than what I ask you to do. Anticipate nothing. Analyze nothing. Just follow my instructions and let the words flow over you, and don't try to help in anyway.

Trust yourself and your inner mind and say out loud exactly whatever comes up, whether it makes sense or not. Report everything that comes to mind. Then there is no way that you won't have a wonderful Past Life Regression experience.

If after Past Life Regression is over and they present this question, you can answer it by asking if they remember when you asked questions during the regression and they said that they didn't know the answers, such as the name of someone, or their age, or the year. When you see them nod their heads, you can ask, *"How hard would it have been to make up a name, an age, or a year? That should be a pretty easy thing to do, shouldn't it? Yet since you didn't know the answers to those questions in hypnosis, it seems to me the answers you did give, that you actually knew them at some level, that they have some meaning to you, instead of simply making them up."*

It is not your responsibility to judge what they should make of the things that came up in a regression session. If they still doubt, you can ask them, *"So what's the purpose of making that up in that way, for your unconscious mind?"* Inner reflection is what they need in this moment.

The other commonly asked question you may want to address before you start a Past Life Regression session is – **"Can everyone be hypnotized to a past life?"**

Everyone can be hypnotized to a past life as long as they stay curious about being hypnotized to a past life; as long as they don't hold a belief inside them saying that they can't be hypnotized to a past life. I cannot hypnotize anyone who doesn't think I can hypnotize them. Curiosity is the key.

Throughout the entire intake, intersperse affirmations into your conversation:

17

- It is easy for you to remember your past lives.

- You want to know and understand the events and emotions and experiences that occurred in your past lives.

- You can remember everything that is important for you to know and understand about your past lives.

- Your past-life memories will help you in your present life.

- Your past-life memories will give you insight and understanding.

- Your past-life memories will help you understand the origins of events that are occurring now in your life.

- You are able to remember and understand all the events and emotions that you experienced in your past lives.

- Your past-life memories open up naturally, and as they open up, you become aware of them and understand them.

When I lead group Past Life Regression sessions, I use these, modified for use in the first person, as an affirmation for the group to repeat after me, out loud or silently, at the beginning of a session.

A musician sent an email to me after participating in a one-hour long Past Life Regression group session: "I got home tonight to google some stuff around the images and information I got in the regression tonight -

and I was BLOWN away! ... Again, I would have no way of knowing this!

I just *had* to share this information with you, Kemila! This is so very exciting! And interestingly enough, even *before* you started to regress us, I was already hearing the sound of an Arabic 'nai', a middle eastern musical instrument, that immediately made me think I was going to find a life time in that region... I found that I was already seeing images of the life time *before* the regression began!

This is such fascinating stuff! I truly look forward to the next one you will do!"

CHAPTER 3

Confidence Building Exercises

The majority of people who go to see you probably have not had a direct Past Life Regression experience before. After the intake, it's time to let them know what the experience will feel like for them in a direct way.

Some people receive impressions visually, they "see" things; some people hear; some feel and sense; some people just have a direct knowing. There is no wrong way to experience a Past Life Regression. However, if they are not visual, and yet they have an erroneous idea that they are not doing it right because they don't "see", that could hinder their experience. Even though they receive a lot of information, they may dismiss it because they insist on one "right" way to receive it. Therefore, at this point, focus on building their confidence first.

There are many creative ways to build a client's confidence. What I normally do is to first guide them going to a favourite place, so that I can observe directly, or get an idea from them afterwards, how they receive impressions. I'll say words such as, *"I'd like you to go to a favourite place in your mind's eye."* When I say that, I'll close my own eyes, and take some deep breaths as a suggestion to the client. They usually follow suit.

Continue letting them know they have complete freedom to select the place and location without judgment. It could be anywhere indoors or outdoors, anywhere that they have been to, a place that they want to go to, or an imaginary place. Ask them to go there and nod their head when they are there.

This is the moment when their inner mind starts to guide the session. An interesting thing is that at this moment, you can learn a lot about this person, sometimes more than the whole intake talk combined.

Some people may battle between two places, which may be the same as when they enter a Past Life, instead of one, they have two competing scenes. In this case, simply tell them, "Pick one, any one. Know that we can always come back and visit another at a later time."

While they go to their favourite place, guide them into the experience:

> *We are moving towards there now. And you'll be open to receive the vivid impressions from this location.*
>
> *Focus on it. Feel yourself moving around there. Be open while you visit this favourite place. Take a deep breath in. Allow yourself to receive the impression on this place. More and more vivid impressions, let it flow, absolutely you are able to receive vivid impressions. Look around and examine*

the surroundings. How does it look to you? (Some people are very in tune with their experience. They may think this is a question to be answered, and they'd answer it, which normally quickens the process beautifully.) *How does it sound to you? How does it feel to you? Take a few moments, looking around, listening, noticing, sensing and feeling. Pay attention to how you perceive. Allow it to flow. There is no need to second-guess. I'll be quiet for just a moment as you explore this favourite place. Now allow the impressions to flow, and pay special attention to how you receive the impressions, seeing... sensing... feeling... hearing... or just knowing...*

After a moment of silence, instruct the client to let go of the image of this place, take a deep breath and open their eyes.

First ask them how they received impressions. Did they *see, hear, sense* or just *know* them? This prepares you for using their organic language. I have found this is a better way to know them than executing a Representational System Inventory[1]. This also gives them an opportunity to know if they are primarily visual, auditory or kinaesthetic. Later in

---

[1] *Representational System Inventory* is a questionnaire designed to help a person discover his/her primary representational system and the first representational component in many of his/her strategies of learning. By knowing it, he/she will be able to understand how he/she takes in information under different situations.

this chapter I'll discuss how this may potentially serve as a transition to a Past Life scene directly.

Check how their experience was. "Was it easy?" After they confirm it, let them know that Past Life Regression is exactly the same type of experience, no more, no less. It is as easy as what they just experienced. It's just another time, another place, maybe in another body, living another life, but how they receive impressions remains the same. Often at this point they will nod their head knowingly. Don't be surprised if your client is already in trance at this point.

Occasionally a client will say that the favourite place imagery was not very easy. Then you can ask what would make it easier. They may say, slower would be better, or they may give you other clues. Whatever they say, use it. And confirm with them that sometimes it's not so easy to start with, but as they tune in, the information flows more and more smoothly and naturally. At this point, guide them one more time, back to the favourite place, and add one more element to it.

> *… Let's expand this a little further. This time I want you to pick a favourite object in this favourite place. Maybe it's a picture, a painting; it can be a flower, a seashell, a rock, or a gift of some kind. It doesn't matter what this object is. Allow yourself to step closer to this object, now. More and more clearly you can see it, closer and closer. You can reach out your hand and touch it. You can absolutely feel it. You are with this object. You can look at it from different perspectives. You can see,*

*and feel the density. You can touch the object.
Notice the colours, the temperature. Is it cold? Is it
warm? What are the textures? Can you feel the
weight of it? Do whatever you can to sense this
object now. You are with it, letting go of all other
thoughts, and focusing only on this object, and
absolutely allowing yourself to be there. You're
touching it. You are there with this object....*

Again, ask them to let the scene go, open their eyes,
and ask how easy it was to experience the favourite object.
After they have confirmed it was relatively easy, you can say
a Past Life Regression is no harder than this.

*Past Life regression is as easy as the
favourite object in the favourite place. It's just
another time, another place, living another life in
another body. Yet how you receive impressions is
exactly the same way. The information is already
there ready to flow. All you are doing is opening up
to your natural ability to perceive the impressions,
which you now know that you do all the time.*

With that you can ask them if they are ready for
another journey, to another place and time, to receive the
images they seek, the images they can learn from.

Converting to a Past Life Regression

Occasionally the favourite place imagery is all it takes
for a client to drop into a deep trance, from which you can

go to a Past Life directly. When you notice the trance happening, do not have the client open their eyes and start a lengthy induction. Instead, convert the favourite place imagery into an induction.

Ask where they are, inside or outside, in this favourite place. If it's outside, ask what is there. Quite often, a client picks a nature scene, a sandy beach, or a place with trees and grass.

If it's a forest or a garden, tell them to continue to walk there. You can engage all their senses. Have them feel the warmth of the sun, see the colours around, hear the silence, smell the freshness in the air, and feel supported by the earth with each step they take. Then ask suggestively if they notice a little river or a stream. The intention is to have clients make this up, but very often clients will be delightfully surprised and ask, "How do you know?" As they go along the river or stream, they will notice, ahead of them, a bridge crossing the river. Then they realize, with your suggestion, that this is a river of time.

Guide them slowly crossing the river of time. I often count from 10 backwards to 1 as they cross. Tell them at the count of 1, they will reach the other side of the bridge, in another time, at another place, maybe in another body living another life. When they start to cross the bridge, bring out some fog, some blue mist, to disorient them, so that when you count to 1, the fog clears up, and they find themselves at the other side of the bridge, in another life. (See the script *Crossing the Bridge of Time to a Past Life* in chapter 5.)

You can also create "a hidden path" in this forest to lead them to a Past Life.

Similarly, if they are at a beach for their favourite place and drop into a nice trance, ask them to continue to walk and enjoy the moment. Tell them that ahead of them, when they look now, is a foggy area. *"It's bright and foggy."* When they get closer, they notice it's a sort of blue mist. Have them go through the blue mist, and when you count backwards from 10 to 1, the fog clears and they will cross time and space to another life…

Sometimes a client's favourite place is indoors, such as home, and they drop into a trance. What you can do is to have them turn on a TV, and watch a Past Life unfold there. Or you can have them get so relaxed that they take a nap and have a dream. In the dream they find themselves flying out of a window, flying all the way up to the sky, to the clouds up high. Then ask them to come back to Earth from the clouds. Tell them when they land, they will find themselves in another place, another time, living another life in another body. You can count backwards from 10 down to 1 to assist them with their journey back.

The key to converting favourite place imagery into an induction is that deep trance is demonstrated by the client at the moment they are in the favourite place. Otherwise, you should do a proper induction and deepening.

One of my clients spontaneously went to a Past Life place when I asked her to go to a favourite place. When I heard her say the favourite object was a blue rock, I had a hunch

27

that she was already in a Past Life, so I simply asked her, "What's your name?"

"Jade." She said in a childlike tone. Since that was not my client's name, we simply started Past Life Regression that way.

Another client went to a church for the favourite place. The way she described the church made me feel it must be old. It turned out she was a boy visiting that church in the thirteenth century.

Sometimes a client may drift to a childhood favourite place and they may verbalize where they are. In that case, you can simply use an Age Regression technique and speak to that child, then move the client further back to another earlier memory, and eventually move them back to a memory from their mother's womb, and then to a past life. For details, see chapter 5 - *Age Regression to a Past Life Regression.*

CHAPTER 4

Induction

I won't spend much time reviewing induction since hypnotherapy practitioners already have considerable experience in this area of basic hypnosis. I will, though, share my first time go-to induction for most clients.

The induction I use is "Finger Spreading". I like this quick induction because it builds in hypnosis agreement, hypnotic suggestions, and tests whether they are a "Direct" or an "Indirect" suggestibility type.

Finger Spreading Induction

The induction goes like this:

As you may know, all hypnosis is self-hypnosis. It is made through consensus, which means you go to hypnosis by making an agreement. The agreement to be hypnotized is easy. It is done by shaking hands. May I (Reach out your right hand, and then continue after they have given you their hand.) *Thank you for making the agreement with me today to be hypnotized...*

Then unexpectedly flip their hand, with the palm facing in front of their face. Use your right hand to make sure that their fingers all stay together while supporting their elbow with your left hand. Ask them to focus their attention on the tip of their middle finger and tap on it a few times to assist that focus. Then say:

> *In a moment, I'll let go of your hand and*
> *your elbow. When I do, you might start to notice*
> *that something interesting is going to happen, that*
> *your fingers will start to separate.*

Let go of their hand and elbow and continue with the patter, "*Separating, separating, wider and wider, further and further apart…*" You can point out that their breathing has shifted, while their fingers continue to separate, wider and wider without them thinking about it. They just notice it.

If their fingers stay tightly closed, they probably don't take in direct suggestions easily. In that case you can say to them:

> *You do not have to make them spread apart,*
> *but do not try to stop them. Concentrate and allow*
> *things to take place. Feel them spreading apart now.*
> *Automatically spreading now. It is beginning to feel*
> *as though there was a string tied to each finger*
> *pulling them apart. Separating further, and wider…*

After a while, and it doesn't matter where they are, you can take their arm and relax it back down, testing as you do so, how much they have let go.

Then, very silently, you pick up the left hand and elbow, and do the same thing. Only this time you are silent. You will tap on the tip of the mid finger again for them to know, indirectly, that they are supposed to focus their attention on it.

You then just let go of the hand and elbow without saying a word. If the fingers separate more than the other hand did while you were giving them instruction, they are probably more an indirect type of suggestibility. If their fingers stay the same when previously they moved a lot, they are a direct type of suggestibility. If the fingers on both hands separate, congratulations, you've got a natural somnambulist to work with. I have not met a person whose fingers don't move at all on either hand. If you do meet one, you may need to undertake initial work to understand the resistance.

After observing their second hand, you can say:

> *Imagine, if we are to install a magnet on your facial area today, so that you can start to attract what matters to you into your life, new opportunities... job offers... a meaningful relationship, confidence, clarity, ease and comfort...* (Try to use whatever is relevant to the individual client based on information you have previously gleaned.) *It will all start by you observing this. So, now, just observe carefully. And tell me, is it your hand that feels like moving closer to your face? Or is it your arm that is moving, causing the hand to move along?...*

(Then regardless of whatever they say.)
That's right. Let it keep coming, closer and closer…
As you always know how it starts when you have a
focus. This is how it starts, your hand (or arm)
coming closer. Feel the magnetic pull, pulling the
hand (or arm) closer and closer to your face, the
same way new opportunities… job offers… a
meaningful relationship, confidence, clarity… closer
and closer. The closer the hand (or arm) comes, the
stronger the magnetic pull you can feel…

Very soon, the skin will touch between your
fingers and your face. When that happens, your eyes
will close and that will be your sign to go into a
deep hypnotic relaxation.

When their fingers touch their face, take the hand, test
the relaxation, and drop it back to the lap or chair.

This induction is followed by any deepenings and / or
progressive relaxation that you typically use. Occasionally,
with clients who find it hard to let go, I use Dave Elman's
somnambulist deepening.

This is also a moment when you can further educate
the conscious mind, to allow the unconscious to flow easily,
by saying:

A lot of people second-guess how they
perceive impressions. Each of us is different. A sense
of the environment, a fleeting image, an emotion or
feeling… Be open to it, because this is how you
receive impressions. And open up all your five

senses to re-experience whatever comes up. Trust that. How you do it is how it is supposed to happen. We can always analyze, think about, and talk about it later, after we have the material to think about and talk about.

As the scene unfolds, you may not understand in the moment, but understanding or head-knowing is knowing about... from a distance.... Heart-knowing or direct knowing is the end of keeping any distance... That's what you are here for. Any impression you receive is IT. You may think you are making it up, because it is beyond rational mind understanding when you are experiencing it, but that's the nature of heart-knowing. There is no need to make sense of anything in that very moment. What's important is to allow what's happening to happen and be able to speak it out loud, because you can remember everything, every experience you have ever had.

Today we may go to visit a Past Life, or we may simply have an imagery journey. I'll guide you. There's nothing for you to understand or figure out as we go along. We will talk about it later. Now it's your time, and I want you to enjoy and experience fully the journey that you are taking. Whatever you see, hear and sense, you will be able to speak out loud. Your conscious part of the mind can take a nap for the coming hour or two, because it will function better in analyzing and understanding afterwards. But during the process, *there is nothing to think about or analyze. You will just say out loud as you see, hear or feel. No judgment is needed, no second guessing is necessary, only experiencing as memories unfold themselves. Your conscious mind can pay attention to a few things, but your unconscious mind can pay attention to everything. Your conscious mind may be listening to my words, but your unconscious mind is listening to how I'm saying them, while you find yourself deeply in the story.*

This is also when I tell them that during the session, the main purpose is to collect data. You can refer to any recording that you or your client will make of the session. After the data is collected (recorded), they will have enough material to analyze, think about and rationalize, as much as they like to, to satisfy their conscious mind.

Bright Light Visualization

Some people like a sense of being protected by white or coloured bright light, or just the comfort of it. This can also serve as another deepening. It never hurts to deepen again, and again.

I'll count from 5 down to 0. I want you to visualize a ball of bright light coming down from above, with the colour you choose – what colour is the light? (wait for an answer.) *Visualize the ball pulsating, which may create a feeling of tingling, heat or coolness.*

5… the bright (the colour they see) *light now at the top of head, the crown chakra* (for people who you know this word would make sense)

4… coming inside your body, from the top of your head, into your mind, because you can remember… let it spread slowly down…

3… It completely relaxes every muscle, every nerve, every organ – all of your body, the torso, the arms, the legs… to the toes…

2… You feel a deeper state of relaxation and peace… more and more peaceful and calm.

1… Let the light fill your body, each space, each corner, each muscle.

0… Breathe more light into your heart area with each inhale now… It forms a ball of (whichever colour) *light there. Now with your next exhale, send out the light into the outside world. Surrounding you, like a cocoon, a shield, or a halo, at arm's length, is this positive, healing energy of* (whichever colour) *light.*

Suggestions to the Unconscious Mind

Now the client is almost ready to explore one of their past lives. Speak directly to their unconscious mind. The parenthetical text in the script below should be adapted to the specific situation that you are working with.

_____ (client's name), *your unconscious process has already started, because it knows why you are here today, because I asked you questions and you gave me answers. Not only did I listen, so did your unconscious mind. While we had a conversation, your unconscious mind already started the process, like a computer, to find the right time, right place, and the right life that you have lived so that you can have the right answers and insights to help you move forward with more ease and trust and comfort and joy* (or confidence, love... whatever you feel will best serve your client) *towards your dreams in this life. You are here today because you are ready, your conscious and unconscious mind are both ready. We have the unconscious mind on board today to help us work on resolving some fears and anxieties and resistance* (tie into the client's agenda). *While the process is going on subconsciously, it will guide us to the exact moment in another life when we reach the right door* (or cross the bridge, land back on Earth again... depending on what you plan to do to transition into a Past Life scene) *today.*

You can experience or relive the experience in regression, experience or relive whatever is going on, or if you choose, at anytime, you can sit in a theatre, watching on a movie screen in front of you, you can watch but not experience it. You can bounce back between the two of you, as many times as you like. This helps you to go even deeper.

As the scene unfolds, don't worry today if it is a memory, a fantasy, an imagination, or a combination of any of those, because your subconscious will take you exactly to where you need to go. Honour it. (Plant the purpose of what the client wants to explore here.) *Maybe your unconscious mind even wants to take you to an historical event that you have lived and can be validated by you later on.*

All kinds of deepening should be used whenever you see fit, as the mind fluctuates with different types of brainwaves. Even when a client goes into a deep trance for a moment, it doesn't mean that they will stay at the same depth all the time. When in doubt, always deepen.

CHAPTER 5

Entering a Past Life

There are many ways a client can enter a Past Life scene. This chapter presents a number of standard scripts for Past Life Regression inductions to help you guide clients to a Past Life experience. Apart from these, however, it is really up to your imagination as to the way you guide a client to a Past Life.

Going Downstairs and a Hallway of Many Doors

This is one of the most commonly used methods, for its clarity and simplicity. Going downstairs is a typical hypnotic deepening. Clients are given enough time to drift into a deeper trance. I usually use 10 steps counting down. Sometimes when I perceive a client needing more time; for example, the finger spreading was delayed, I would count down 20 steps instead.

> *Visualize or imagine yourself standing at the top of a beautiful staircase. It may be one of the most beautiful staircases you have ever seen. You*

can feel the soft texture of the luxurious carpet beneath your feet. You feel the freshly polished wood of the handrail, and you decide that you are ready to walk down the staircase to explore one of your many past lives.

There are ten steps, and as you hold the handrail and I count from ten down to one, simply allow yourself to double your relaxation with each step you take, so that by the time we reach the bottom, you will be totally, completely, absolutely limp, loose, and relaxed.

10… double your relaxation as you move down one step.

9… slowly, easily, one step at a time

8… doubling your relaxation yet again

7… enjoying this feeling of warmth and peace and total relaxation

6… drifting down even more now into total relaxation

5… you are halfway down now, enjoying this wonderful, tranquil relaxation

4… another step down into this wonderful peaceful state

3… more and more relaxed

2… almost there, and

1… feeling totally relaxed now as you step off the staircase

Very occasionally, a client prefers going upstairs. I had a client, who due to some trauma, was afraid of basements. Moving downstairs implied a basement for him, so going down was not a feasible direction. Also going upstairs can create a sense of moving away from Earth and into the cloud, which is nice imagery for Past Life Regression. When moving a client upstairs, say to the client, *"Your body is so relaxed here on this couch, so your mind is relaxed as well. As your conscious mind is relaxed, your subconscious mind is free, free to travel through time and space. So in a moment, you'll be drifting up the stairs, one step at a time, moving, drifting, rising, floating up."* This way, you avoid tiring the client by walking up the staircase.

After they step off the staircase, you can use the imagery of a hallway to visit one of their Past Lives.

> *Right in front of you is a beautiful hallway. It is so long that you can't see the end of it, with large and magnificent doors on either side. These are doorways into your past. Each door represents a lifetime that you have lived. As I count backward from 5 to 1, one of these doors will somehow appeal to you, a door to your past. This door will attract you. It almost feels like this door is pulling you. When you feel it, go to that door, because it contains some answers to the questions you seek today. Behind that door are some scenes to be revealed to you that are very important for you to learn.*
>
> *Do not worry about what is imagination, fantasy, actual memory, symbol, metaphor, or some*

combination of all of these. It is the experience that matters. Just let yourself experience whatever pops into your mind. There is no need at this moment to think, judge, or critique. Just let yourself experience. Whatever comes into your awareness is fine. You can analyze it later.

5... Going down the hallway, peacefully, calmly.

4... One door starts to get your attention. This door will help you to understand (the presenting issue) *in your current life. Go to the door. Go all the way to the door. Trust the process.*

3... You are at the door. Put your hand on the doorknob. The door is opening, opening...

2... You are ready to be in another time and another place. When I say "One," be there on the other side of the door. Let it all come into focus on the count of one.

1! Be there.

Quickly the first impression, daytime or nighttime?

Inside or outside?

First impression, are you alone or are you with someone?

Crossing The Bridge of Time to a Past Life

As I mentioned in Chapter 3, crossing a bridge over the river of time can be used to convert the favourite place imagery directly into a Past Life Regression. But it is also a good induction to be used alone.

... Feel completely drowsy and sleepy and completely relaxed. Let every muscle, every nerve relax. Now feel this relaxation. Good... At this moment, you can start diving deep into your unconscious mind where all the memories of your past are stored, so that you will be able to go back, back beyond this life, beyond the womb of this current life, to where you are in another body, in another life. You may choose to focus on a significant, important Past Life, which you are willing and ready to know now. The all knowing self within you knows about this significant Past Life memory.

Trust now, as I start counting backwards from 10 to 1 (or 20 to 1 if more time is needed; or 5 to 1 if the client shows signs of readiness). *I want you to know, you will be crossing the bridge, the bridge which crosses the river of time. As you walk cross the bridge and walk to the other side of the bridge, you will be there, in another time period, in another life, which is significant and important for you to know now.*

10... Be there now, at the bridge. Send out... your consciousness, your mind, which can travel, across this bridge. Easily gently step onto the bridge when you are ready...

9... There you are... stepping onto the bridge. When you look ahead, you can see a lot of mist ahead of you... It's kind of foggy, so you can't see the other end of it, but you trust this process.

8... It's safe to go back to this significant... Past Life. It's important for you to now know. All your guides and masters and your higher self are with you invisibly. You are safe and protected.

7... Continue with the journey... back in time. The closer you are to the other side of the bridge, the closer you are to those memories.

6... Trust. Much deeper and deeper... You can vaguely pierce through this mist. The mist gets cleared as you start walking through it.

5... Halfway there... As you slowly reach the other side of the bridge, the moment you step off the bridge, you are there, in that significant Past Life.

4... Now the mist is getting clear. It's much clearer than the other side of the bridge which you just left behind.

3... Almost there... It's very clear. By the count of 1, step into the scene on the other side of the bridge, and step into those memories.

2… Without analyzing or editing, allow yourself to be there, in that memory, in that life.

1… Step off the bridge into the scene. Quickly, daytime or nighttime?

Inside or outside?

First impression, are you alone or are you with someone?

…

Bring your attention down to your feet. Notice, what kind of footwear you are wearing…. (Go slowly. Be attentive and observant of their facial expressions. You want to give them time to absorb their surroundings without allowing them to conclude that they are not succeeding in entering a Past Life.) *You can feel, you can see, you can trust impressions that are coming to you now, about your footwear…*

Through the Rainbow and Down to the Earth Chamber

This guided rainbow imagery is a very beautiful experience. It's suitable for people who are imaginative and/or who are metaphysically oriented. As this script is quite lengthy, some people may not wait till the end to have some Past Life experience; therefore it's good to set up an ideomotor response[2], such as asking a finger to rise when some memories spontaneously come through.

I also use this a lot in group Past Life Regression sessions because it's quite soothing, pleasant, and general. In group settings, I tell them we are going to go through each and every rainbow colour before we enter the earth chamber to a Past Life. And I always remind them that we each carry a rainbow within us, within our body – That's what they call the seven colours of the chakras.

Refer to the preceding script *Going Downstairs and a Hallway of Many Doors* for material to use if a client prefers going upstairs. You can use it in place of the earth chamber in this script.

> *In this pleasant state of relaxation, imagine, picture or visualize yourself out in the country. You are walking over a field of lush, fresh grass. The air is clean and pure. It is a gorgeous day, and the sky is a radiant blue with just a few fluffy clouds high up in the sky.*
>
> *You walk along, and you now notice that ahead of you is a magnificent rainbow. You feel excited as you have never been this close to the foot of a rainbow before. It smells refreshing and clean. The colours look vibrant and pure. A shimmering*

---

[2] Ideomotor Response (IMR) relates to involuntary bodily movement or unconscious motor behaviour, especially when it's made in response to a thought or idea rather than to a sensory stimulus. It is an exploratory method used in hypnotherapy to uncover unconscious material.

spectrum of colours that blend one into another and it's the most beautiful rainbow you have ever seen.

You walk right up there, to the rainbow, until you are standing so close that you could touch it. When you look up, the rainbow appears to go straight up into the sky. You reach out to touch the rainbow, and your hand goes right through and into the red area. Your hand feels slightly tingly, warm and secure, and you realize that the red is making your hand and arm relax even more.

It feels so good, that you decide to step inside the rainbow. When you look around now, all you can see is red. Red in front of you, behind you, on either side of you, above and below you, and as you are totally bathed and encircled by this gorgeous red, you feel your mind becoming more and more aware.

It feels so pure, so restful, so quiet, and yet so comforting. All you can think of is red, red, red… (pause)

Now you feel yourself moving on with a few steps forward, until you find yourself entering the orange area. The red felt so comforting and relaxing, but that was nothing compared to the utter tranquility and peace of the orange. You breathe in this orange colour, which makes you feel that you are standing on the earth and in the sky at the same time. The gentle orange permeates every cell of your body. You are totally surrounded by orange, and *you are also part of the orange as it is inside every cell of your body. You are nothing but pure orange, orange, orange…*(pause)

The desire to explore further comes to your awareness, and you take another few steps forward until you are in the colour yellow. You are familiar with the colour yellow, but you have never experienced a colour as perfect and serene as this one. You feel your mind opening up more and more, becoming more and more aware, expanding and increasing…. Surrounded by pure yellow, yellow, yellow…(pause)

You begin to move more easily through the colours now, and you are ready to walk through into the green. The vibrant, healing energy of the green almost takes your breath away. You feel restored and invigorated in every pore of your being. Relax and allow the green to move into every cell of your body. This makes you feel more in touch with your inner feelings. Oh, this centre point between physical and spiritual energies of green, green, green…(pause)

It's only a few steps until you're completely surrounded by blue. As you enter the colour blue, you feel peaceful and very tranquil. You experience a wonderful sense of knowing and understanding that the sky and the earth are really one and the same, with no difference between the universe and yourself. You look around, entranced by the wonder of this majesty of blue, blue, blue… (pause)

And now you are moving inside the healing energies of indigo, a deep purple-blue. You feel better than you've ever felt before, as you breathe in the colour of pure awareness and true inner knowledge. You feel your mind completely opening up and expanding into what's beyond, and you're enjoying the feelings of deep peace and contentment as you gaze around at the magnificent indigo, indigo, indigo... (pause)

There is only one colour left to visit. You're eager to move on to violet, but you retain all the feelings you felt while experiencing the wonderful qualities of the other colours.

And now it's time to move on. One step, two steps, and three. You are now surrounded by the spiritual qualities of violet. You feel it spreading into every organ of your body, restoring your body, mind and soul. The colour violet opens up your mind's awareness even further with more understanding of your spiritual nature. You enjoy its soothing tenderness and gentle awakening of your spiritual centre. There is something indescribable about violet, violet, violet...(pause)

And now it is time to leave the rainbow behind. You feel reluctant to leave, but you know that the rainbow is just a foretaste of what is to come. So now you step out of the rainbow, and back onto the luscious grass of the field. You find a nice, pleasant spot to lie down, you take a long deep breath in, and you let it out slowly.

So you are now totally relaxed in every nerve, fibre, muscle, and cell of your being. You are limp, loose, and so relaxed. You have experienced the nurturing energies of each colour of the rainbow, and now you are ready to return to one of your Past Lives.

Ahead of you, you notice an opening in the ground with stairs descending into the earth. So you move ahead, and now you start to descend the stairs, one by one, until you find yourself in a luminous chamber below the ground. Now going downstairs. I'll count for you, starting from 20, one step at a time, going down the stairs, 19, all the way down, 18, 17, ... 3, 2, 1, 0. You are standing now in a luminous chamber. In this chamber there are many doors. Each door represents a lifetime you have lived. You can choose any lifetime to visit simply by walking up and opening one of the doors.

5... going to the door that appeals to you

4... getting closer

3... putting your hand on the door knob

2... pushing it open, see the light coming out of it

1... opening the door, and stepping into it!

0... first impression, daytime or nighttime?

Inside or outside?

First impression, are you alone or are you with someone?

Look down at your feet. What are you wearing on your feet?

What are you feeling in your body? Focus on your inner vision.

Age Regression to a Past Life Regression

Dr. Brian Weiss has laid out these methods in some of his best selling books. I don't use them a lot for two reasons. First, the purpose for a pleasant meal recall (see the following script) is to build confidence, which can be achieved by doing the favourite place imagery. Secondly, it can be a lengthy process going back to childhood and it is possible to get stuck on a childhood memory and not be able to pass it to go further. Even though it may be therapeutic, it may not serve the client who comes to see you clearly stating that they want a Past Life Regression experience.

There have been times when I have had a client reach a childhood memory, which is not necessarily unhappy, and they feel overwhelmed by emotion. One such example is recalling the love that was demonstrated by a now deceased relative. The client is reluctant to move on from this positive or joyous recollection yet it was not their original goal. Other times a client can be spontaneously regressed to a childhood trauma. As a therapist we deal with what happens. When this happens, you can tell your client that their unconscious mind has wisely led you both to what you actually need to address, in this case, a past memory in this life.

51

For these reasons, I generally don't use this method if the client is clear that what they want is a Past Life Regression session.

If a client comes to see you for the resolution of a problem, then you can't necessarily predetermine where the problem originates. You have to go where the unconscious mind takes you. In this case, *Age Regression to a Past Life* can be an ideal method, because it can uncover possible sensitizing events in this life.

> *First, let's just go back and remember the last pleasant meal that you had or a wonderful dining experience. See where it was; when it was; what you ate; who was there with you.*
>
> *What does it look like, taste like, smell like, and what does it feel like? If there's conversation going on, what does the conversation sound like? Use all of your senses, because you can remember… completely. Remember your feelings. If you have the full memory with you now, raise this finger to me… Now drop it and go as deep as you can, because you can REMEMBER…*
>
> *Relax even deeper. Hypnosis is only a form of focused concentration. You never give up control. You are always in charge. If you ever get anxious while having a memory or experience, I'll touch your arm like this, and you can just float above it and watch from a distance, like watching a movie.*

What you'll see and sense today are only memories, like any other memories, just like you remembered the pleasant meal. You are always in control.

When I count from 5 to 1, we will go back to an early memory... 5, 4, 3, 2, 1. (Choose one of the following depending on the situation.)

A. go back to your mid teenage years, around the age of 15. See what you can remember from then that has significant meaning to your (presenting issue).

B. go back to a time from which your (presenting issue) arose.

C. go back to a happy or pleasant memory from your mid teenage years... you can remember some of the clothing that you were wearing... what are you wearing... what do you see... that pleasant memory... what does it sound like, smell like...you can even remember what your shoes look like... when you have that memory, lift this index finger...

Then count them back to an earlier memory. It could be about age 8. After memory recall at that age, you say:

Now we will go even further back. Don't worry what is imagination; what is fantasy, what is metaphor or symbol, actual memory or some

53

*combination of all of these. Just let yourself
experience. Do not let your mind judge or criticize
or even comment on the material you are
experiencing. Just experience it. This is only for the
experience. You can critique it afterward. You can
analyze it later. But for now just let yourself
experience.*

*So when I count from 5 to 1, go even earlier
in memory, you were just a little baby, because you
can remember.*

You then count them to a babyhood memory. After
that, you can regress them back to the womb.

*When I count again backwards from 5 to 1,
go back to the memory of your mother's womb. You
can use your imagination to remember what it is
like in the in utero period, just before you were born.
Whatever pops into your mind is fine. Just let
yourself experience it. Listen to the music of her
stomach. Access your mother's emotions. If you
concentrate, you can know a thought or feeling she
may have towards you…*

You can either choose to allow the client to be verbal
or non-verbal here.

Hallway to a Past Life

After the womb experience, have them imagine
something they didn't notice before. At the backdoor of the

womb, is a beautiful hallway or a corridor with magnificent doors. You can either refer to the script *Going Downstairs and a Hallway of Many Doors* at the beginning of this chapter, or use the version below:

> *Now at the back of your mother's womb, there is a door opening, a wonderful long corridor with many doors. Sweeping away in front of you in a long gentle curve... so that you can't actually see the end of it, but you know instinctively that it's completely safe... Go through the corridor. One of the doors will be pulling you close to it...and as you move along the corridor, you see bright light shining through the door that pulls you...*
>
> *Now you are standing in front of the door. I'm going to count down from 5 to 0. At 0, you will be in another place, another time.*
>
> *5... Put your hand on the doorknob.*
>
> *4... Push open the door.*
>
> *3... Opening, opening...*
>
> *2... Almost there. You will be able to speak out loud and still remain in this relaxed state.*
>
> *1... Step through the door.*
>
> *0... You are there now.*
>
> *Is this daytime or nighttime?*
>
> *Inside or outside?*
>
> *Are you alone or are you with someone?*

Through A Tunnel into a Past Life

An alternative to the previous *hallway to a Past Life* at the back of the womb is for them to notice a dark tunnel instead. They can't see what's at the end of the tunnel yet. The tunnel leads to a significant Past Life that they have lived before. You can use a count from 20 to 1, moving the client through the tunnel, using the following script:

> *You notice that there is a tunnel, at the back of your mother's womb. This tunnel will lead you to a significant Past Life, where you will find the information that would be the most helpful for you in the discovery and healing of the issues we have discussed. This is most valuable for you today in discovering the root cause and the means for healing the* (presenting issue) *you have been experiencing.*
>
> *I'm going to count from 20 to 1. As I do so, feel yourself moving through the tunnel. You will find yourself moving through this dark tunnel that will get lighter and lighter as I count backward. When I reach the count of one, you will reach the end of the tunnel and find yourself in a Past-Life scene.*
>
> *Now 20… you are moving into a very deep tunnel, feeling calm and comfortable.*
>
> *19… it's quite dark so you feel a little bit disoriented, but you know where you are going. Allow your inner memory to guide you.*

18... you don't need to know what you already know. You allow things to unfold for you only when you reach the end of the tunnel.

17... you're moving backward in time, back, back, back...

16... keep moving back, you are doing great...

15... Continue...

14... 13... moving so far back...

1... continue the journey...

11... 10... you are halfway there, the tunnel is becoming lighter...

9... that's right, that's where you are going...

8... trust the process...

7... 6... you can almost see the end of the tunnel. Yes, that's where you are going...

5... nearly there, you have made it...

4... when I count to 1, be there and let it all come into focus...

3... almost there the end of the tunnel...

2... and 1... be there!

Is this daytime or nighttime?

Inside or outside?

Are you alone or are you with someone?

Moving through the Universal Light into a Past Life

There are some people who are interested in a non-physical experience as much as or more than a Past Life Regression. For these metaphysically oriented people, going to the universal light can be either a prelude to a Past Life or a full experience in its own right.

Age Regression to the back of their mother's womb can be a good starting point from which you can take someone directly to the universal light. This works because the universal light is representative of existence before birth or beyond physical life. Many people describe this experience as, "Just light, everywhere. Warm, but not burning, very loving and peaceful."

When immersed in this light, some people may feel reluctant to speak with you for a long while. Give them time and space to experience it. Gently guide them and let them know there is no immediate need to communicate with you and that they can take whatever time they need. In hypnosis, clients can be extremely sensitive to a hypnotherapist's impatience.

However there are other techniques you can use to take them to the universal light besides Age Regression to the womb. In some cases you can skip Age Regression and take them directly to the womb by asking them where they were at the time of their birth. Alternatively, you can avoid the womb entirely by floating them up to the universal light according to the script *Floating up and Down to a Past Life* which follows next.

Once someone is in their mother's womb, you can take them to the universal light as follows:

> *When I count from 5 to 0, move backward through your mother's womb, into your spirit being surrounded by a beautiful white light. 5, 4, 3, going back, 2, 1 and 0. You are now soul energy… Step into the universal white light and let it surround you. Allow your energy to float around in the light. Feeling free of your physical body… Let yourself relax and be at peace.*

When people go to the universal light, they experience a non-physical existence, in which they may also have other metaphysical experiences. These can include meeting their deceased loved ones, spirit guides, spirit helpers, masters, angels, the elders, the council, etc., or finding their soul mate in the spirit world. However it is difficult to categorize people's experiences, as they are often very personal.

People may have difficulty describing the experience, as our language belongs to the physical realm. Using physical language to describe non-physical or metaphysical experiences can be challenging for some people. Nevertheless, their facial expression can express their awe, or their internal process.

When people tell you that they are in communication with a person or being while in the universal light, it helps to give them space to experience this by saying: *"If you need to receive and process some message, it is your choice whether to do this privately or to share this experience with me. If you choose do so privately, take your time, and raise this finger when you're done."*

All sorts of metaphysical experiences can happen in the universal light, depending on the individual client and their needs. This experience itself can take a whole session, which can be an awe-inspiring experience, or it can take a short while as a segue to a Past Life. In the latter case, you can follow their time spent in the universal light with:

> *In a moment, you'll feel a gentle tug on your ankle, pulling you slowly and comfortably, to land back on earth, because when your feet touch the ground, you will be at another place, at another time, in another body, living another life. It will just happen naturally. Your subconscious will take you on the exact journey that you are supposed to go on, perhaps the lifetime that has the most valuable information for your life today. I will count from 20 to 0, and at 0, you will be at another time, and another place.*
>
> > *20… feel the gentle tug on your ankle*
> >
> > *19… going down to*
> >
> > *18… 17… going even deeper and deeper...*
> >
> > *16… going lower*
> >
> > *15… 14… all the way down*
> >
> > *13… 12… drifting down deeper*
> >
> > *11… 10… half way here now*

9... looking down below you, starts to become clear at

8... beginning to become a little clearer, coming down with

7... 6... starts to come into view

5... 4... imagine or visualize your feet land on the ground

3... almost there

2... remaining relaxed

1... you are landing, and

0... touch the GROUND. Look down at your feet. What are you wearing on your feet?

Is this daytime or nighttime?

Are you inside or outside?

Are you alone or are you with someone?

Floating up and Down to a Past Life

For people who report having had Out of Body Experiences, or for those who have vivid flying dreams, this is an excellent Past Life Regression induction. It's direct, easy, relatable, and no nonsense. Because of its neutrality – taking a person up and down doesn't imply a direction in time – this can also be used for Future Life Progression[3].

---

[3] *Future Life Progression* is to visit a future time - either the current life in the future or a future lifetime - in hypnosis.

You can use your imagination to imagine or visualize, here today in my office, as you lie on this couch, what your face looks like, your mouth, your jaw, your neck, your shoulders, your arms, hands and fingers. Go ahead and make a picture of yourself, real and solid, what you look like, lying here with your eyes closed, so relaxed. You can look at your chest, your stomach, hips, legs, ankles, and feet, all your body... Now use your imagination, as if you are floating up, looking down at your self-image on the couch. Floating up higher to the ceiling, looking down, at me, the chair I'm sitting in, the desk, the other furniture... the entire room... now imagine or visualize you are floating up so high...visualize outside the window... float up even higher... see the streets, the traffic, where are those people going? (Depending on where your office is located, you can put real things here, such as forest, beach, fields, well-known landmarks, etc.)

Float up so high that you can see the whole city... Continue to float up higher now, and you can see the whole province, the coastline, beautiful waves, the Pacific Ocean (Substitute geographical information specific to your locale) *... Floating up so high, you can see the mountains, snow capped tops... slowly up and you can see the outline of the continent, all of the North America, all the land... Let yourself float up so high that now you can see what the astronauts see – the beautiful blue Earth,*

62

so blue, with clouds, the Earth slowly spinning
beneath you, so big, but so small...

   Float up so high you are now in the centre of
the universe. Without gravity I really don't know if
you look down, look up, or look sideways when you
look towards the Earth. Where you are now, there is
no time, which means time is like a mountain range.
All of time exists all at once; with past, the present
and future simultaneously existing, all on a single
plane...

   With perfect trust, because you are safe and
secure and you have all the tools, in this serene
tranquility, give yourself permission to go further
into the journey...

To use this script to take someone to the universal
light, you can follow the preceding with:

   Getting brighter now... You are now soul
energy... Step into the universal white light and let
it surround you. Allow your energy to float around
in the light. Feeling free of your physical body... Let
yourself relax and be at peace.

To float back down to Earth to another lifetime, use
the floating down portion of the previous *Moving Through the*
Universal Light script.

Fantasy Clothes Store to a Past Life

This Past Life induction is suitable for those who have excellent imagination, who like history, and who treat Past Life Regression as tourism rather than therapy. It's good for recreational use and hence for group sessions, though therapy can certainly happen. I once had a client whose profession was costume design for TV productions. She was thrilled by this Past Life induction.

Start by asking some hypnotic questions. These questions are meant to provoke clients into searching deep for answers. As such, the answers may be important for the clients themselves, but may be of little interest to you as a therapist.

- *If you could win an all-expenses-paid trip to any country in the world, where would you most like to go?*

- *Have you ever read any stories, fact or fiction, about (their selected destination)? What are they?*

- *Do you enjoy watching movies or TV programmes about (their selected destination)?*

- *Do you happen to know anybody from (their selected destination)? What are your feelings towards them?*

- *What foods do you associate with (their selected destination)? Have you ever tasted them… and do you like them?*

- *List any particularly strong feelings, either positive or negative, you may have experienced when you were imagining* (their selected destination).

- *Do you have anything in your home – furnishings, rugs, ornaments, pictures etc. that remind you of* (their selected destination) *for any reason?*

- *Do you remember any particular types of games you played as a child?*

- *Did your family members tell you about anything unusual you did as a child?*

- *Have you every experienced déjà vu? Where were you and what was your emotional response to it each time?*

And then continue with the following script.

Allow your mind to drift, close or far, even miles away, maybe to a vacation spot, because while your conscious mind drifts miles away, your unconscious mind is always here, curious about the journey that you are going to embark upon. We are going on the journey by feeling a pleasant, relaxing warmth throughout the body first... The conscious part of the mind can feel happy to TAKE A BREAK, NOW, if it wants.

With your eyes closed, allow yourself to go, breath by breath, into the deep, deep core of your being, a central essence... that essence is non-physical, exceptionally enduring, possibly immortal, and has existed for thousands of years before your present life.

This is the fundamental you. Now get in touch with that essence of who you are, because that essence, which is totally beyond your everyday consciousness, has memories to share, stories to tell. The personality of who you think you are has lived for some decades. Yet the essence of you has the experience of perhaps thousands of years to draw upon, all stored in the subconscious memory bank.

The way the essence of you has gained this experience has everything to do with what we normally think of as reincarnation. It creates personalities as the focus of its attention. Such personalities are 'sent' into incarnation to learn and experience. Now, for this moment, I want you to withdraw from the familiar personality and dive deep, deep within you, because every life that you have ever lived, the information is still there, locked up in the deeper strata of your mind.

Creative fantasy does not produce something out of nothing. If you think you are making things up on the go, just keep making things up and enjoy the unfolding.

So now, imagine yourself entering a very special kind of clothing store. It is an endlessly big store, and it carries on its endless racks clothes from

every country and every region in the world. Even
as you enter the store, the sheer variety of choice is
bewildering, for you quickly notice that not only is
every country and region represented, but clothing
from different time periods is also on display. Here
is a true panorama of fashion through the ages, from
every culture in every clime.

As you enter, and stand there bewildered,
you realize in a moment, you will find some
costumes that feel right for you; and you know
when one feels right, it has nothing to do with how
you know yourself to be in this life. As a matter of
fact, the moment you walk into the door, you check
in at the doorway your jacket, umbrella, hat, other
accessories, and your personality. Also, there are no
restrictions for your body type, your gender, or your
age. That's how a costume can feel right to you. It's
as if your body can automatically fit in to that
costume, when it feels right.

The proprietor of the store bustles across and
greets you as if you were his most honoured
customer – perhaps you are, since, in our fantasy,
you entered this store carrying an American
Express platinum card with unlimited credit.

"I have just the thing for you," says the
proprietor who starts to lead you through the store.
As you follow him, you feel like you are walking
across vast time and space, all the way into a nicely
carpeted private changing room at the back. On the
walls are full-length mirrors. Next to them is a

walk-in wardrobe. It is towards this wardrobe that the proprietor is pointing.

You walk to the wardrobe and open it. Displayed inside, is the costume the proprietor has recommended for you out of his vast selection of clothes from every country and every age. You carefully take it out of the wardrobe, and examine it closely. You know this is the costume that feels right for you. In the mirror, it's going to reflect a new you, a new image, yet it looks so familiar. The light in the change room dims, you put the costume on and the light begins to become bright again. You study yourself in the mirrors...

Look at yourself in the mirrors, from the different angles. See the style and material in detail. Whatever image you see there, it's all right... Now, how do you feel the first moment you saw the costume? How do you look in it? What country or time period did it come from? What does your hair look like? Facial characteristics? While you wear the costume, are you aware of a mood change in yourself? Any particular emotions, feelings or attitudes?

Can you spot any linkage between the way the costume makes you feel and your current attitudes and reactions?

As you look into the mirror and see your own reflection, a new shape has taken form inside the mirror. The image is so strong that you try to

reach out to touch it… and as you do it mimics
your movements… and you realize this image is
you… but from another time, and another place…
As you get closer, the shape becomes clearer and
sharper. And as it clears and sharpens, you go down
deeper and deeper into relaxation, feeling safe,
secure… watching the mirror… seeing the shape
become clear… seeing what's happening now in the
mirror…

> *Are you male or female?*
>
> *What colour are you wearing?*
>
> *Describe what you are wearing.*
>
> *How old are you?*
>
> *Is anyone with you?*
>
> *Are you inside or outside?*
>
> *Is it daytime or nighttime?*
>
> *Speak out loud and tell the story of what is*
> *going on. What is happening around you?*

In general, a mirror can be an excellent tool to use in Past Life Regression. When you take a client into a Past Life scene, if they can tell you daytime or nighttime, inside or outside, but they don't know what they wear on their feet or body, you can introduce a full-length mirror into the scene, and ask them what they see in the mirror. This can help a client visualize themselves in a more objective way.

Movie Theatre Viewing of One or Multiple Past Lives

This induction is good for people who, for some reason, are afraid of experiencing embodied Past Life memories. This offers them a relaxed way to review a Past Life from a distance. It's also very flexible and versatile as it can be used to view one Past Life, or multiple Past Lives. In this theatre, the client holds a remote control so that they can feel in charge of what they see and experience.

Additionally, when viewing a Past lifetime, if you sense the time is right, you can float the client from sitting in the theatre, into the screen to experience the Past Life directly. This then becomes a regular Past Life Regression.

First guide the client going downstairs. At the bottom of the staircase, the client enters a private theatre, where the client can sit in the centre seat, feeling comfortable and relaxed…

> *Now you can relax even deeper in this soft, luxurious, comfortable chair. You notice you are here all by yourself, so you feel safe to open up to the show. There is nobody else here, only my friendly voice. And you understand my friendly voice is here to help you with what you are going to experience, to guide you from time to time, and to support you.*

> *Right in front of you, is a big screen. You know in this private theatre, this screen is going to show you, in the greatest clarity, with the absolute truth, your deepest subconscious Past Life*

*memories. It may show you one or more Past Lives
that you have lived before. You will be in control.
Now you look around the room, the light is dim,
you can barely make out what's here, but you know
this theatre is a theatre by you, for you.*

*I want you to reach down beside the chair.
When you do so, you are going to feel an object and
I want you to pick it up.*

*Now look at your hand, and you see that you
have a remote control.* (Normally the client
naturally nods to acknowledge it. If not, you
can further ask to reinforce this, *"Are you
holding this remote control with your right hand or
left hand?"* They will give you an answer,
which serves as an acknowledgement.) *This
remote control has ON and OFF buttons, Fast
Forward and Rewind buttons, a Pause button,
Increase Volume and Decrease Volume… just like
your normal remote control. You realize this remote
control is for the big screen in front of you. In a
moment, when you turn it on, what you are going
to see on the screen is a scene, you will be able to
know what's happening as it happens, you will be
able to follow the story, and you will be able to
answer questions at the same time.*

*On the count of three, push the ON button.
Let the scene unfold. 1, get ready; 2, and 3, push the
button on…. What you see, merging out of the
mist, is…*

Daytime or nighttime?

Inside or outside?

What is happening? Allow everything to come into focus.

Whenever you would like them to move backward or forward in time within a Past Life, or to jump into another lifetime with the same theme, for example, the same emotional problem, ask them to use the remote control fast forward or rewind button to do so.

As an alternative to a Past Life Regression, this method can also be used to regress a person into their pure spiritual state, their soul, or their higher-self. Instead of having a scene unfold when they push the ON button, have an image of them in their pure spiritual state be projected on the screen in front of them. After they've described what they see, invite the image to speak through the client's voice. Because the image they see on screen represents their own pure spirit being, and it is in a sense themselves, it now becomes easy for the client to give a voice to their soul or higher-self.

Being in this state provides them a great opportunity to both answer questions about their current situation or presenting issue, as well as questions that span multiple lifetimes. These latter questions can be rewarding when a client has already had Past Life Regression experiences. Examples of these types of questions are:

• how many lifetimes they have lived

- the proportion of male and female lives they have had

- the geographic locations and eras they have lived in

- the relationships they have that span lifetimes.

Affect Bridge to a Past Life

Affect Bridge is a technique for the hypnotherapist to guide the subconscious mind of the client to regress to a past experience that is of significance to the present problem. As the name implies, the Affect Bridge technique forms a bridge between affects. This is useful when you are working on locating the root cause of a client's problem, and when strong emotions are present and demonstrated by the client in your office.

The Affect Bridge technique can be used in Past Life Regression as well as Age Regression. As an advanced technique, you should have previous experience or training with regression and with dealing with emotionally charged situations before using it. The client can often enter the regression at a traumatic moment filled with very strong emotions.

There are multiple aspects to Affect Bridge and they require the hypnotherapist to be fully present with what's going on with the client. The windows of opportunity for regression sometimes only open very shortly before the conscious analytical mind kicks in. Therefore you really need to be present and engaged with the client and can't be reading a script when you use the Affect Bridge technique for regression.

After inducing the hypnotic state, ask the client to bring up the feeling and describe it. It can be an intense feeling of a fear, such as fear of water, fear of height, or fear of spiders; it can be anxiety, such as social anxiety or performance anxiety. Sometimes a you can pick up a word, a phrase, or a sentence from their description that you can use as a reference to the feeling or emotion. For example, a client with anxiety about the future may express their anxiety as, "I will run out of luck and bad things will happen to me." By using the direct intense feeling, or a feeling associated with the reference word, phrase, or sentence, you can ask the unconscious mind to regress to the first point in time where this feeling was felt. This normally puts the client right in the situation, in which the subconscious mind learned the problem-state.

There are different aspects to the Affect Bridge technique as mentioned above. One aspect, Somatic Bridge, focuses on the physical sensation of a painful emotion. Another aspect, Linguistic Bridge, focuses on the language a client uses to describe their emotions. Below I first discuss how to use these individually to conduct Past Life Regressions. Following that I describe several ways to combine both the Somatic and Linguistic bridges to create a complete and holistic Affect Bridge technique to a Past Life. The discussion of Affect Bridge concludes with a brief outline of how I combine Somatic Bridge with Tunnel

Visualization to take a client directly from their presenting issue to that issue's initial sensitizing event.

Focusing Directly on the Sensation in the Body - Somatic Bridge

Somatic Bridge gets the client to focus directly on the sensation they feel in their body when they think about the feeling or emotion. Ask the client to locate the sensation of intense painful emotion in their body. Once they have located it, get them to focus on the sensation. Use the script below to help them objectify and experiment with the feeling so that they gain a sense of control over it. When they have learned some control over the objectified sensation, you can use the technique to regress them back to previous sensitizing events.

> *Give it a colour. What colour is this sensation? Now give it a shape, a shape that reflects the discomfort. What shape is it? Give it a size. See how big or small it is. Now notice that you can make this shape larger and smaller. As it grows larger, so does the sense of discomfort in your body. As it decreases in size, so does the discomfort. Experiment with making it larger... and smaller... Now I want you to reduce it in size so that you can sense only a mild feeling of the discomfort.*
>
> *Allow your mind to drift back to other occasions when you felt this discomfort or when you were aware of your fear or phobia. You are still in*

control of the shape and you can reduce it in size if
any of the memories become too painful.

Take time at this stage and see how many occasions in the past – it could be this life in the past, or a Past Life – that the client can remember when they were affected by the fear or phobia. Allow the sensation in the body to build and grow.

Take a deep breath in and exhale slowly. You
are now going to enlarge the shape, which will
increase the feelings of discomfort in your body.
Allow the shape to grow as large as you can stand,
and then allow yourself to go back to the very first
time you ever felt this sensation, when I count from
5 to 1.

After counting from 5 to 1 the client should be at the event that initially sensitized them to the feeling of fear or anxiety. Encourage them to allow the story of that event to unfold. Note that this may be a traumatic scene that they step into, and that you will often be dealing with intense emotions.

Focusing on the Language Used to Describe the Feeling - Linguistic Bridge

Linguistic Bridge gets the client to focus on a word, phrase, or sentence that they use to describe their feeling or emotion. This can also be called "Verbal Bridge". Because everyone uses language in their own way, you can utilize a verbal bridge to access memories in the unconscious. When a client speaks about issues in their present life, you can listen for key words or phrases that trigger or are associated with their anxiety or fear. These are often, but not necessarily, frequently used phrases. However occasionally the important phase may be rarely uttered and it can take patience and practice to identify it. Once you have identified a word or phrase, you can use it as a way to access the unconscious without taking away the presence of the conscious mind. Request that the client close their eyes, concentrate, and repeat the phrase until additional phrases arise or a mental image appears as an earlier sensitizing memory.

> *Keep repeating* (the word, phrase, or sentence e.g. "I just can't live up to others' expectations."). *A story will emerge. It may be from this life or another. Repeat the words, again, and again, and let them take you into a scene that they bring up* (Notice the intensity of the emotion as the phrase is repeated by the client. If intense emotion is absent, Affect Bridge regression cannot be achieved.)...*that's right, let your unconscious take you to a story when something like this happened... where are you? And what's happening?*

Again note that this may be a traumatic scene that they step into, and that you will often be dealing with intense emotions.

Putting It All Together - Affect Bridge Technique

The complete Affect Bridge technique combines aspects of both the Linguistic Bridge and Somatic Bridge to get to the sensitizing event, which may be either in this life or a past one. It is a very powerful hypnosis healing method.

One way to combine Linguistic and Somatic Bridges is to first get the client to focus on the sensation or feeling in their body as described previously. At the same time identify a key word or phrase that they associate with the feeling. Once you get a word, phrase or sentence associated with the feeling or sensation, you can ask the client to repeat it out loud, again and again.

Ask them how they are feeling, where they feel it (or where they feel it most strongly if the feeling has multiple locations). You can even instruct the client to put a hand there, so it keeps them charged with that phrase or sentence. Observe the intensity of the feeling. Ask the client:

I will count from 5 backwards to 1, and at 1 you will get images of the very first situation you had when you felt this feeling, and you had the thought that _____ (key word, phrase, or sentence e.g. "I am not allowed to use my power.").

Go back in time, 5…, 4…, 3 to the place and time where you _____ (again repeat the words or phrase. e.g. "are not to use your power."), *2 and 1. Let the images come. Feel the* _____ (certain feelings. e.g.

sadness) *at your* _____ (the body part that feels it. e.g. heart area.). *Where are you and what is happening?*

To help them become anchored in the scene, you can also use typical regression openers such as *"daytime or nighttime"*, *"inside or outside"*, *"are you alone or are you with someone"*.

Another way you can combine the Somatic and Linguistic bridges is to ask a body sensation to speak. This creates a more direct Affect Bridge approach. It is achieved by having the client talk about the region of their body that embodies the sensation or feeling as if it could speak. In other words, they give that sensation a voice. This helps ground the client in the experience that is bringing about their thoughts and feelings. When a client is feeling anxiety or fear, allow them to feel the anxiety in their body, and to breathe deeply into those feelings. Then have them speak the very next thoughts that originate *from* the feeling. By continuing to have them focus on the feeling and verbalizing its thoughts, they can eventually lead you to the sensitizing event.

Feel the feeling on your (the body part that embodies the feeling or emotion e.g. the chest). *Imagine that it can speak. What does it say? Keep talking from your* (body part). *Give it a voice. Be aware of any thoughts that are reinforcing this belief that... What else does it say? Whose voice is this? Where are you now?*

Most likely, you will be engaged in a dialogue with the body part. Your goal is to guide the discussion through Age or Past Life Regression to the sensitizing event.

Combining Somatic Bridge with Tunnel Visualization

Something I often do is to combine the Somatic Bridge technique with a visualization of going through a tunnel - See *Through a Tunnel into a Past Life* in this chapter in the subsection on Age Regression. The Somatic Bridge focuses on the clients issue and a Tunnel Visualization is a great way to take people to another time and space. Together they provide a technique to go directly from the presenting issue to its initial sensitizing event.

First have the client focus on a feeling and have them locate the sensation in their body – it could be a physical pain, or a certain emotion, as long as they can feel it in their body, it will be fine.

After they locate that sensation in their body, have them objectify it – to give it a shape, a size, a colour, a density. After the sensation becomes an object, ask their awareness to go inside the centre of this object. From the centre, they perceive that a long tunnel starts to extend, leading towards the first time they ever felt this way.

From the centre, you notice there extends a long tunnel. You can't see the end, but in a moment, you will be moving along the tunnel, all the way. I'll be counting for you, from 20 to 1, and you'll be moving along the tunnel. Go all the way. Where the

tunnel ends, is where the _____
(sensation, pain or emotion) *starts. Go all the*
way. When I reach the count of 1, you'll be at the
end of the tunnel. Entering the scene that has
everything to do with why you are here today.

20, 19… (This can be the same as the *Age*
Regression Tunnel to a Past Life.)

Miscellaneous Past Life Regression Inductions

The Past Life Regression inductions presented in this section are not full scripts, but instead are short, partial scripts or imagery suitable for clients who don't need lengthy inductions to access Past Life memories. What's listed in this section can be good for people with whom you have worked before, or those who show you the signs of deep trance easily and quickly. Also, you can use these mini-inductions as ideas to stimulate your imagination and create your own scripts.

A Relationship Connection

This partial script is useful for those clients seeking to explore, in past lives, their relationships with people who they know in their current life.

You are in a deep state. In a moment I am
going to count backward, from five to one. You will
be in a deeper state and will feel totally safe. Your
mind will be free to roam back in time, back to the

time when the connection to (a person in their current life) *began, back to the time that had the most significant bearing on what happened between you and* (him/her), *back to the time and space where you meet* (him/her) *before. Allow the unconscious to scan for precise moments or lifetimes of any previous relationship between you and* (him/her), *regardless of the sex or who may have been whom in that life. When I say "one", you will go back to that lifetime and remember it. It is important for you today to understand, to know, and to grow. You can do that. I'm going to count backwards and tap you on the forehead. When I say "one", you'll see where you are. The information will be shown to you. Five… four… three… two… one! Daytime or night time?…*

Heading Downward in a Water Park to a Past Life

This is a fun induction but make sure that the client is not afraid of water or heights before using it. I've used it in times when clients come back wanting to review the same lifetime they have visited before but in greater detail, as this script gives them overt control of where they are going before they start to move to a past life.

Now visualize or imagine you are out there in a large water park. There is a large chute, like a water slide. At the top there is a handle. By turning this handle you control the Past Life that you will emerge into. Test turning the handle now… In a moment, when I count from 5 to down to 1, you feel

82

that you have turned the handle in the right direction. You will sit down on the chute and enjoy sliding back into that Past Life.

Now turn the handle, when I count from 5 to 1, you will find the right direction.

5... 4... 3... 2... 1... that's right. That's the one.

I want you to slide down the chute, while I count from 10 to 1, I want you to enjoy sliding back into the Past Life that your subconscious mind has already chosen.

10... start going down

9... 8... going down further to that lifetime

7... 6... pick up the speed, faster now

5... halfway there

4... almost there ...

3... 2... 1... there you are! First impression, daytime or nighttime? ...

The same idea can be used for a client using a time machine. When they set the time that they are going to visit, the time machine will start automatically and transport them to the chosen lifetime.

Elevator Down to a Past Life

Similar to the caution with the previous induction, make sure that the client is not afraid of small spaces such as an elevator before using this induction.

Now imagine yourself walking into a beautiful elevator. As the door slowly closes, you push a button as I slowly count backward from five to one. The elevator will travel back through time and through space. The door will open when I say 'one' and you will step out of the elevator into another scene, another time, another place, in another body, living another life.

Get ready. Take a deep breath in. And push the elevator button now.

5... The elevator is moving

4... back in time

3... through time and space

2... almost there

1... Now the elevator stops, and the door opens. Take a deep breath. Step outside, and join the scene, and experience...

Where are you? Outside or inside?

Daytime or nighttime?

Are you alone or are you with someone?

A Path in Garden to a Past Life

The garden visualization is commonly used as deepening in hypnotherapy. It is very relaxing, and you can utilize all of the clients' senses: beautiful flowers, green grass; fragrance in the air, taste of freshness; sunshine on the skin, breeze; birds chirping, the quietness; and the softness of earth in each step they take.

You can create a hidden path leading to somewhere else for the client. On that hidden path, you can guide the client to a past life by counting from 10 to 1, after walking through a blue mist - See Chapter 2, *Converting to a Past Life Regression.*

Or, after following the winding path, the client can come to a hill with steps going up, or an opening in the earth with steps going down. After that, the client comes to a door. Have them notice the details of the door. They can even verbalize what the door looks like – size, colour, thickness, material, decoration, etc. Then they gently push (or pull) open the door. Inside the door, is nothing but white light. When you count from 10 to 1, they will travel through the white light to another place and another lifetime.

Then you count from 10 to 1, while they travel through the white light as a person travels along a highway, to another lifetime that they have lived before.

River Banks

One of my clients went to a river cruise in Asia when I asked her to go to her favourite place. That inspired me to create this induction for some people.

*Imagine yourself on a small boat, making its
way down the river of life. You can steer the boat to
shore whenever you wish, because wherever you
choose to stop, it will be an important occasion in
one of your Past Lives.*

Recurring Dream to a Past Life

There are times when a client reports a recurring
dream that they suspect may be a Past Life dream. It's very
easy to have them go back to that dream in the trance state.
First do a Progressive Relaxation, asking each body part to
go to sleep in turn. For example you can start by asking the
toes to go to sleep, then the feet, ankles… all the way to the
head areas, so that even the conscious part of the mind is
relaxed and ready to go to sleep.

*While your body goes to sleep, the mind goes
along into a deep sleep-like state. And when you
sleep, you dream. I know that because when I sleep,
I dream too. It's a natural thing to dream during
sleep. And when you dream, you are free. Free to
travel through time and space, through dimensions
and realms. As I speak, you find yourself going all
the way to that dream – you know, your
unconscious mind knows which dream I'm talking
about. That's right, that dream where you…*

You can then elicit some elements of the dream that
the client has shared with you, in detail, so that you help the
client vividly recall. It is important for you to continue to use
the present tense when speaking with them. Ask them to

describe the dream. Continue to get them to describe what they experience next. Even though the dream may have ended at the same spot each time in the past, in hypnosis, the story can continue. That way, you can use the dream to induce a Past Life Regression.

Library Book Opening to a Past Life

You can use guided imagery to take a client into a big library and have them feel drawn to a section of books in which their name is printed on the bindings. This can be an added delight for people who like books, especially those who like libraries. Each book represents a Past Life that they have lived. You can then have them open the yellowed and frayed pages of one book, and on the right-hand side of the open page is a coloured plate, almost like what one would find in a book of fairy tales. Then have the client tell you what the picture shows.

After that, you can instruct the client to go into the picture when you count from 3 to 1. The story can then unfold there.

Keys to a Successful Past Life Regression

During a Past Life Regression information gets expressed in small pieces moment by moment rather than remembering as a full story. It is very rare for a client, at the moment they go into a Past Life, to say things like, "Okay. This life is about such and such. The story starts like this, then it develops in this way…" If you meet someone like that, you can start to think that this person may be making things up.

On the contrary, a story in a Past Life Regression can unfold and develop very slowly. There are moments that a client is actually not quite sure what is going on, and they can start to doubt if they are doing it right, or if they are really hypnotized. In those moments, a Past Life Regression therapist's timely guidance is very important. Leave enough gaps for them to experience and report what is going on, but not enough for them to doubt.

Constantly encourage them that they are doing it right by saying, "that's right", "very good", etc. This encouragement can be very comforting for the client, especially if it's their first time doing Past Life Regression. Sometimes, when a client doesn't know the answer to your question, you need to reassure the client that it's okay not to know the answer now, and give them a suggestion that it will come easily to them at a later moment. Then you move on.

As a Past Life Regression therapist, you must demonstrate confidence. Your tone of voice is very important. Leave no room for doubt in your voice when you ask these initial questions:

- Is it daytime or nighttime?

- Is it inside or outside?

- Are you alone or are you with someone?

After you ask those initial questions the client may want to jump ahead and try to make sense of everything. Remind the client to just focus on answering questions. It's not their job to make sense of anything during the experience. This is the same reason to project confidence with your voice, to help the clients unconsciously answer the questions and keep their analytical mind at bay during hypnosis.

Tapping on the forehead when asking the questions helps them focus; or simply drop their hand each time you ask a question. It creates a distraction for the conscious analytical mind.

Sometimes a client may search around for the answers. To the third question "are you alone or are you with someone" they may say, "I don't know." You can gently coach them through by saying something like, *"Because it's daytime, you can allow yourself to see, feel or know if you are alone or with someone."* Or *"I know it's nighttime, but after a while your eyes get used to it, so you'll know or even see."*

If they give answers, you can move on. Even if they don't, you don't want to dwell on these questions and pressure them too much. That could create a sense of failure in them, or they could start to think that they are not doing it right. Both can cause them to begin consciously thinking about their experience which is not what you want to happen at this moment. Instead, you can gently coach them:

> *That's all right. It'll all come to you clearly in a moment. But now you can look down at your feet... Are you wearing any footwear on your feet?*

Most of the time you will get an answer. Then ask:

Are you standing, sitting, walking or lying down?

Mostly, they'll say they are standing. Now you can repeat back to them what they are wearing (or barefoot) and ask:

What kind of surface are you standing on?

That question leads to environment checking. You can find out what surrounding they are in. You may come back to this moment, this location later in the session, because many times the entering scene has some significance for a soul's psyche.

At some point as you are establishing the entering scene for a Past Life, ask about the clothes they wear, whether they have long hair or short hair, and if it's long hair whether the hair is worn up or down, and whether they are wearing a hat or not, as well as their hair colour. These types of questions can help lead to identifying their age, gender and race. They are also simple enough to answer, and at this stage, getting information is still secondary. Your primary focus is still building confidence that they can experience a Past Life, and that they are doing it right.

While doing environment checking, it's not unusual that a client will say, "I don't know. I can't see anything." Again, they may think "seeing" is the only way to experience a Past Life Regression. In this case, you can shift their attention from an insistence on "seeing" to another sense. For example, *"You can hear sounds, or maybe quietness, when you listen, really listen. What do you hear?"* Often times, this can anchor them with what's going on in the environment. For example, after shifting her attention and then pausing, I had a client say, "I hear children laughing." With that anchor, she moved herself to a window, looked out to a backyard, and noticed two kids playing there. At that point, "seeing" didn't seem to be a problem anymore.

You can continue to encourage clients each step of the way, by saying things such as:

> *At this moment, I'd like you to describe what you are experiencing. This experience deepens more and more as time passes... At every point of time, during the experience, you can talk to me, you can tell me about what you are feeling and experiencing. As you verbalize, go into a very deep transparent state, deep into that experience.*

After this initial stage, it's up to you as a therapist how to move forward. If the client shows any emotions at this moment, it may be wise to allow the emotions to guide where you need to go, such as previously discussed for *the Affect Bridge* technique. You can also simply ask how they are feeling and thinking at this moment, and again, allow the emotions to tell the story.

In some cases, clients feel neutral. They still don't know what to make of everything. In this case it helps to guide them to a place that is often familiar. Tell them:

Now I'll give you a keyword. This keyword is 'home', the place you sleep at night. When I count from 3 to 1, be there.

3, 2, 1, now you are at home. Describe it to me. Are you outside the home, or inside?

(If they are not sure) *Now you are at home, but you haven't entered it yet. You are standing right in front of it, a sort of doorway. 3, 2, 1, you are there now. What are you aware of?*

I have found that guiding them to move through the door and go inside step by step has made it easier for them to explore.

After exploring their home, if a story hasn't developed yet, guide them to a mealtime. It's a good way to gather information about their family members, and from what they eat, the utensils they use, and the lighting source, you can also get some sense of geographic location, or time in history.

You may also ask if they can find a mirror anywhere at home. Then ask them to go and look at themselves in the mirror. Some people are able to describe clearly how they look as if they are right in front of the mirror; some would say the skin colour, hair colour and age, but the face is vague. Either way, encourage them that they are doing excellently.

Dealing with Nervousness or Resistance

Even though the initial questions are answered, during the process, the clients' conscious mind may still take them out of the trance, and at some point they may go "blank". You need to get and keep the conscious mind out of the way.

Fractionation can serve as an excellent deepening in this situation by surprising them and asking them to open their eyes. Then say to them:

> *Since it is obvious that you sincerely want the truth about yourself, you can break through the barrier in your mind. No matter how bad it has been, it is okay for you to know now, because the truth will always help you to be free. Now today we are going to find out more about* (their presenting issues). *This is obviously important to you, and your all-knowing mind knows exactly* (what they are seeking to discover).

Say this in the most sincere way. I normally find their head nods as I speak. With their eyes open, you can also notice their trance stage. Then instruct them to close their eyes again, or to close their eyes whenever they feel comfortable to do so. If you have set up re-hypnotizing suggestion beforehand – such as *"each and every time, when I count from 5 down to 0, at 0, your eyes will be closed if you haven't done so, and you'll go into a deep state of hypnosis, each time deeper."* – then simply count from 5 to 0 to create eye closure again.

If they start to see things within the Past Life but then begin to try and make sense of what comes to their awareness too soon and ahead of the proper time, distract them by saying:

> *The mind always wants to make sense of what's going on. Yet that same mind doesn't really have the memories that we know we have on a deeper level. Your body has its intelligence, and certainly the body has memories. For example, I am speaking to your index finger on the right hand now. If you hear me, this finger of yours, just lift it and let me know…* (wait till the finger rises.)
>
> *Now you can use this index finger of the right hand, to give yourself permission to honour your subconscious mind, that you will trust the journey that the subconscious wants to take you on, will you?* (again, wait till the finger rises)
>
> *Honour the journey you are about to go on. There is a purpose; we are not just doing a research.*

In Extreme Cases

There are some cases where no matter what you ask, a client will insist that they are not seeing anything. This usually occurs when a client has a strong belief that a Past Life Regression has to happen in a certain way or they have a strong unconscious fear.

In this case, it helps to have the client open and close their eyes a few times (fractionation again). Then say to them:

> *I'll be speaking some words to your unconscious mind. It's not important for you to find answers and reply to me verbally. As I'm communicating with your unconscious mind, your unconscious mind will start to communicate with me by raising this finger, which means, whenever you have an answer, an image in your mind, an idea, a knowing, a feeling, this finger will rise by itself to communicate it. Lift this finger now when your unconscious mind understands.*

After you get a finger lift indicating yes, continue to speak the following script very slowly while paying attention to their finger. This script may not make too much sense to the conscious mind, but overloading can be a good way to hypnotize and deepen in this situation.

> *You said you couldn't see anything… That's very common. For a while there seemed to be nothing there. Nothing, just vacuum - emptiness – blankness. The blankness is nothingness… So allow this nothingness to settle in, that's right, completely allow this blankness, this beautiful blankness to settle in.*
>
> *This blankness is a canvas, because nothing can emerge out of things; things can only emerge out of nothing. That's right, things can only emerge*

*out of nothing. So in this blankness...you can move
freely through your conscious, subconscious and
unconscious, even deeper into your superconscious,
and experience other times, other places, other
selves that you are.*

*Those selves that you also are, live within
the atoms and molecules of your being, and they can
become as aware of you as you can become aware of
them... until in the distance, far away, you see a
shadow appearing. And as the nothing that you are,
at this time, drifts back through time, that shadow
becomes clearer, sharper, becoming more focused...
Let it be a scene... indoors, or outdoors?... Let
them emerge... out of this nothingness... a daytime,
or a night time?*

*Does where and when you are now matter to
your conscious mind? See it or feel it EMERGE
from this complete nothingness... of the conscious
mind? Memories, images, maybe ideas emerge, out
of this blankness, from your unconscious, from your
DEEP inner mind. Nothingness in your conscious
mind is like the quiet surface of a lake. When it's
still on the surface, it gets clear, as clear as this
blank nothingness, that's when we can SEE, what's
there; what has ALWAYS been there, deep down in
the lake.*

*That's right, whatever emerges out of this
nothing, bits of information... memories...
images... feelings... sometimes even a smell, or
sound... You will know when you know...*

something emerges... perhaps it is vague or transient at first... clear it up, little by little... bit by bit.... Impressions... What is it? I wonder. Daytime? Or night time? Inside or outside?...

When you see, when you sense it, you'll know. The sound of your voice will not disturb you, it will just take you deeper, while you are able to communicate with me from your deeper level of the lake. So we can continue to let this scene unfold... A place in time emerges... impressions... presented from the inner mind...

Wherever they are you can guide them down or deeper to a Past Life. Utilize whatever comes as a new induction.

It is our clients' minds that we are working with. Occasionally you will meet someone who is almost determined, unconsciously, that they will not "see" anything. They may, for some secondary gain, be invested in not being able to see anything. In this case, there is likely nothing you can do to change it. In some unintuitive way, a client not seeing anything in a Past Life Regression may actually serve them, at this point in time, even though they think they want it. To have a successful Past Life Regression, both willingness and readiness have to be in place.

When this happens, you may end the session by giving them a post hypnotic dream suggestion:

As you sleep tonight, you'll dream about one of your Past Lives. You'll see the images very clearly, you'll feel deeply, and you'll remember every detail about your dream. In the morning, you'll understand your dream perfectly. You'll interpret it accurately, and you'll understand all the Past-Life connections with your present life. You'll be able to use the knowledge you gain to help you in your regression session, should you choose to, as well as in your present life.

CHAPTER 6

During a Past Life Regression

Now we have reached the culmination of all of the work you have done so far. Up until now you have been gathering information, preparing the client, inducing them into trance, and guiding them into the first scenes in a past life, so that you can conduct a Past Life Regression.

This is the moment you refocus on the issue that has brought the client into your office: curiosity? emotional burden? physical symptoms? spiritual yearning? mental condition? behavioural pattern? relationship exploration? You will accordingly move the client to some significant events that bear on this issue.

The first part of this chapter provides guidance and lists some general questions that you may ask a client in the hypnotic state, regardless of the goals of the session. These questions allow you to gather information about the Past Life and help you move a client back and forth in time.

Following those general questions are sections that deal with specific issues you may encounter during the course of the Past Life Regression, such as a client's resistance to view a specific scene or releasing emotional energy that arises.

The chapter concludes with several advanced techniques that you can use to help clients learn from their Past Life Experience.

Basic Questions During a Past Life Regression

This sub-section presents some general questions that you may ask a client during Past Life Regression, regardless of the goals of the session.

Note that facts such as names, geographic locations, and years, don't matter so much to the soul. Try not to ask about these directly as a person's conscious mind can just make that up, or get frustrated when it is not directly accessible. Find ways instead to ask about these things indirectly. For example, when a person undergoing a Past Life Regression is with someone in a scene, ask, *"Listen carefully. What does he call you? What's your name?"* Or ask them to see if there is a calendar somewhere in the place to tell them the date and year. Having them check their mail is also another way for them to locate their full name and address. People tend to be more confident with answers to basic factual questions when they can simply read the answers from somewhere.

Entering a scene

The following questions are applicable to when a client has just entered a scene of a Past Life Regression. This could be a result of any of the following scenarios:

- when entering a Past Life as discussed in the previous chapter;

- when the setting changes as a result of moving the client forward or backward in time;

- when the client spontaneously changes the setting;

- after a period of deepening if needed by the client.

The goal of these questions is to help the client gain a sense of place and time, to be comfortable within their surroundings, to continue to build confidence in re-living the Past Life experience and describing it to you, and to understand any meaning or importance the scene holds to the overall Past Life. Not all scenes will be of equal significance. However it is important to note that the significance of a scene may not be obvious upon entering and will require gentle probing and patience to bring out.

The questions themselves are only examples of things you can ask. Use your own judgement (and imagination) in deciding which questions and how many to ask. I have listed them roughly in the order that I would ask.

- *Going slowly up your body, note what you are wearing. How does it look or feel? Feel the texture, see the colours...*

- *Do you have anything on your head? Do you have long hair or short hair? (If long,) is your hair up or is your hair down? What's the colour of your hair?*

- *Now, in your mind's eye, slowly look around the place where you are standing and say out loud what you see or feel. Look around and talk about what you perceive. Just let the story tell itself.*

- *What are you aware of? Describe your surroundings.*

- *Look at the architecture. Can you identify where you are now?*

- *What are you feeling right now?*

- *Notice what's happening around you?*

- *Just get in touch with who you are. If not now, very soon, you'll know your name and all about yourself.*

- *I want you to tell me what else you are aware of.*

- *Stay fully in that experience. Tell me what happens next.*

- *In order to move forward, I want you to tell me what's next.*

- *What is the name of the nearest town?*

In an Activity

The following list of questions are examples of the types of things you can ask clients when they are engaged in activities during a Past Life Regression. Life happens when there are activities. It is through activities that you can get a sense of what happened in that life and what has been internalized by the past life personality. You can get an idea of where the problem may originate. Therefore you will know what therapeutic intervention to use.

Even though the clients are in a hypnotic trance, and you are engaged in a conversation with the client in their past life personality, it is still a dynamic and spontaneous conversation, and therefore cannot be scripted. The following are some examples of questions that you may ask; however, your focus is on client. Allow yourself to flow with the conversation and allow the conversation to take you to what needs to surface during the regression.

- *Go on. What's next?*

- *Describe what's happening.*

- *Whatever comes to mind, just speak out.*

- *Concentrate on your breathing and I'm going to ask again. 3, 2, 1 and what comes to mind?*

- *I'm going to count from 3 to 1 and on the count of 1 you'll know. 3, 2, 1.*

- *Tell me step by step what's happening?*

- *All right, now just let that memory continue and just describe what happens.*

- It will become clearer and clearer to you and you will remember.

- You will remember "why" at the count from three to one. 3, 2, 1. What comes to your awareness?

- Describe what you see - Bring the images into sharper focus.

- I'm going to count from 3 to 1 and it will become very clear to you. Just relax, take a deep breath – a really deep breath. Now, exhale and just let out any tension. 3, 2, 1 and what comes to mind?

- Does what is chasing you ever catch up to you? There is a part of you that knows if it's yes or no.

- What are you experiencing? What are you aware of?

- Do you cry out? What would you say if you could let it out?

- Where are you now? Where do you go now?

- I'm going to ask you to concentrate on your breathing. I'm going to count from 3 to 1 and you'll become much more relaxed and calm and your inner mind will let you proceed step by step so that you can see what happens to yourself. 3... just becoming very relaxed as you experience what's happening... 2... 1. What are you aware of?

- Tell me what you say to them. Tell me your exact words.

- *I will tap you on the forehead as I count backward from 3 to 1. Let* (name, place, year...) *pop into your mind, into your awareness. Whatever comes to you is fine.*

- (If they are silent because they are observing something) *You will be able to talk, and yet you will be able to remain in a deep trance state and continue to observe and to experience. What do you see?*

- *Explore and describe your feelings.*

- *What are you experiencing now? What are you aware of right now?*

Moving Forward in Time

Moving clients through time is one of the most common things that you will do during a Past Life Regression. Because a Past Life Regression can be such a unique and intriguing experience for people, it is easy for some to become engrossed in where they are and what they are doing. They will be living in the moment in the past. It is your job to recognize when no more useful information will be gained from their current situation and guide them forward or backward in time to an event from which new insights may be gained.

When moving clients forward in time, I recommend that you use a forward count such as from 1 to 5, or from 1 to 3 in order to convey forward momentum.

- *Okay now. I'm going to ask your inner mind to choose the next important occasion. 1, 2, 3... You are there now. What's happening? And how old are you?*

- *And now I'd like you to just let go of that memory and concentrate on your breathing and I want to ask your inner mind to move ahead to the next important event – something that you need to know about. 1, 2, 3... Be there now.*

- *Move forward now and tell me anything that is important for you to know.*

- *Now I'd like you to move ahead to the next significant event. Your inner mind will select the event we need to look at. 1, 2, 3... What are you aware of?*

- *I'm going to ask your inner mind to take you to the next event and perhaps this is the event that has to do with your _____* (presenting issue or whatever needs clarity at the moment). *At the count from 1 to 5, staying calm and relaxed. 1, 2, 3, 4, 5, what are you experiencing?*

- *When I count from 1 to 5, I want you to move forward in time to the next significant event in this life. 1, 2, 3, 4, 5...*

- *Go on, move forward in time, what happens next that is important to you?*

- *Move forward in time a few minutes to see what happens.*

- *Skip forward to the time when...*

- *You will see yourself when you are older in this life. Tell me what you are doing.*

- *Does anything happen to you in this lifetime that's important?*

- (To another life) *Is there any other life that you feel the same way? Take yourself to that life in your own time, no need to rush.*

Moving Backward in Time

Sometimes the client may enter a scene where they are at an old age. I have had sessions when a client directly entered a death scene. Also there are times that you need to take clients back to an earlier time or even childhood to better understand the overall context or flow of the life. Or the client may discuss an experience, and you want to explore how some of the emotions or behaviours they exhibited came to be formed. In those cases, you need to take the clients backward in time.

When moving clients backward in time, I recommend that you use a backward count such as from 5 to 1, or from 3 to 1 to help convey backward movement. The following are some of the scripts you can use to help a client moving back in time.

- *I'm going to take you back before this day, I'm going to take you to a time when you were ...*

107

- *Go back to an earlier time in this person's history for any clues.*

- *I'm going to count from five to one and you will go back in time a little to just before that event. 5, 4, 3, 2, 1, and whatever comes to mind, just speak out.*

- *Go back to the age of _____, when your parents are still alive...*

- *Locate the source or cause of the condition.*

- (if they are experiencing a strong emotion) *When previously in this lifetime have you experienced this feeling of* (their emotion)?

- *Start again at the beginning of the event. Notice what decisions you are making. Look and see, get a sense. What is your feeling of what is going on? What exactly is happening to you?*

- *Look back over your whole life, and see how the feeling arose.*

Moment of Death

Death is usually a profound experience – undoubtedly a life changing experience. Potentially, revelation is given. Insights can be gained. Mental or emotional fixation can often be released, or carried on, in which case the therapist can help release it. There is always a lot to learn at the moment of death, or a better word – transition.

As in real life, the moment of death during a Past Life Regression can be expected or can occur unexpectedly. An expected death is one that is guided by the therapist, "*When I count from 1 to 3 go to the moment of death.*" An unexpected death is one when you ask a client to move forward to discover a result of something, or simply to move forward some years in the future, and you receive an answer such as, "I don't know because I died before that."

In either case, the moment of death can be very insightful and there are benefits to be had by guiding clients through the death experience. It provides an opportunity for people to gain closure on events that happened during that life, or with people who were significant, and it allows clients to bring into focus and understand lessons from that life.

Care must be taken though because as with any death, it may be peaceful or traumatic. Even an expected and peaceful death can potentially be unsettling for some clients based on their cultural background or personal perceptions surrounding death.

Traumatic death may be associated with fear, anger, or other negative emotions. You can help the client release these emotions by re-living the moment of death. Please see *Releasing energy* in the following sub-section for questions that you can use to help release energy and for a script specific to releasing energy associated with a traumatic death.

The following are questions that you can use to explore the moment of death with clients. Release any charged emotions before undertaking these questions. Also release if charged emotions arise during the exploration of the moment of death. Again, I have listed the questions roughly in the order that I would ask.

- *I'd now like you to go to the last day of this life that we are exploring. You will not have passed over, and you may see the scene in a detached way, almost as if it's happening to someone else, if you so choose. You feel safe to do that. Are you there?*

- *What are you thinking / feeling at the moment of death?*

- *What is your feeling toward…? / What are you thinking?*

- *Do you have a strong physical sensation or pain at the moment of death?*

- *Let's go to the moment of your death, just before your spirit leaves your body. What are the last thoughts you have as you're dying? What are the last feelings and beliefs you have at death? How have those* (repeat the feeling or beliefs) *influenced your behaviour / formed your survival pattern in the life as* (client's name)?

- *And now, it's close, it's within a moment or two of your death…And as you go up… feel it, experience it and breathe … breathe comfortably,*

*easily... breathe comfortably and easily... just
keep breathing... and describe what comes to your
awareness.*

- *Leave that body behind. Leave every sensation
  and every symptom of illness in that body. Leave
  it behind you. That is no longer your body. Leave
  the pain of death in that body where it belongs.
  Leave the sensations of every condition in that
  body as you separate from it. That is no longer
  your body.*

- *What were the events that have resulted in*
  (presenting issue) *in your life as* (client's
  current name)? *What are the significant events
  that contributed to that or caused that? Whatever
  comes to mind...*

- *Now I want you to feel yourself leaving your
  body, are you feeling lighter? Floating like a
  feather, rising up into the air ... Look down at the
  scene you have just left below. What do you see?*

- (Touch shoulder or hand) *It's all over now. You
  can let it go.*

Before Ending or Concluding a Past Life

Now that the Past Life is over and the moment of
death has passed, the client's state of being is in-between
lives. This is a great opportunity to either look back over the
life just lived and see if there are any overall insights to be
gained, or to put that life and the client's current life together
to explore and understand any parallels between them.

111

- *Are there any other important events that you need to look back at?*

- *Looking back, is there any unfinished business in this life you just lived before we move on?*

- *Is there anyone who you have unfinished business with or desire closure with at the moment of death? What would bring closure?* (Explore this with the client as you judge necessary.)

- *Is there anything you want to say to* (a key person the client discussed within the Past Life) *now, looking back?*

- *How does this life relate to your* _____ (presenting issue) *in this life as* _____ (client name) *today?*

- *And now I'm going to ask your inner mind, at the count from 3 to 1, to give you insight about what it is, which incident is related to your problem of* _____ (presenting issue) *in this lifetime?*

- *If you are to put that life as* _____ (client's past life name) *and this life as* _____ (client's name) *together, do you see any parallels?*

- *Was there anything else from that life that is still affecting you in your current life?*

Specific Issues During a Past Life

This sub-section discusses several common and general issues that you may encounter during a Past Life Regression or that may be a result of a client's goals or presenting problems that you discussed with them during the intake process. No life is ever the same, past, present, or future. Therefore there are myriads of situations that may occur in a particular Past Life Regression session.

This sub-section goes into more detail for several specific scenarios. These include when a person doesn't want to go into a certain traumatic scene, relationship connections in past and current lives, and how to release pent up energy. It also presents two advanced Past Life Regression techniques; Mind Merge helps clients see a situation from another's perspective, and and Parallel Reality Regression helps clients understand the power they have when making life choices.

When Someone Doesn't Want To View A Scene

There are times when a client resists viewing a specific scene. It may be because the scene is too traumatic, they sense it is going to be traumatic, they may feel shame, or they simply consider that what would unfold is something they would prefer to keep private for some other reason. People's motivations are incredibly varied and you as the therapist need to discern how critical viewing this scene actually is. Sometimes you may not need to go there, but other times, it can be key to reveal the event for healing to happen.

Once I had a female client who went to a male life in a Past Life Regression session. In that life, he was young, living in a small village. One day, he decided to leave the village and go somewhere else. When I asked for the reason, he said that was what he wanted. I sensed something else going on, but he stressed he didn't know the exact reason...

After probing, and using ideomotor response[4], finally we found out that the young man had a girlfriend, who went to the riverside with him. She wanted to go swimming. He thought it was dangerous as the current was rapid, but he couldn't stop her. She was drowned, right in front of his eyes.

The young man felt so guilty and shamed that he couldn't stay in the village anymore. He thought he was responsible for his girlfriend's death. He blamed himself for not being able to save her. The shame was such that not only did he not want to tell me, but also the real memory was blocked from himself. It was the ideomotor response that

---

[4] Ideomotor relates to involuntary bodily movement or unconscious motor behaviour, especially when it's made in response to a thought or idea rather than to a sensory stimulus. Ideomotor Response (IMR) is an exploratory method used in hypnotherapy to uncover unconscious or repressed material. The most common use of IMR is to ask a client to respond to yes or no questions by finger and/or thumb movement.

helped both of us to know. With that, there came the overdue self-forgiveness.

The following questions can help you probe what is happening in the scene. Be very gentle and compassionate as you question. One thing to remember is that you should never force a client into a scene without assuring them that it is safe and secure to go there. Give them gentle suggestions, such as: *"Let all the tears come out and let all those negative emotions go, so very soon you will feel much lighter, freer, and better."*

Sometimes it may help to skip going through an event as if re-living it, and move directly to the end of the event, from where you can gain any needed information by looking back on it. If you force it, there is a chance that clients will bring themselves out of hypnosis and terminate the session.

- *Why is that? You are being very emotional and shaking your head no. You can tell me. I'm a therapist and I'm used to hearing things. Just feel free to talk about it.*

- *I'm going count from 5 to 1 and at the count of 1 you will find it much, much easier to tell me about it. 5, 4, 3, 2, 1.*

- (with resistance when they say they can't do it). *Yes you can! You can do it. You are not alone. I'm here with you. Tell me what you see. Stay calm and relaxed. Calm and relaxed. It's all right.*

Tell me what you see. You can do it. This is your big chance.

- (When they say they don't want to go somewhere) *Breathe deeply and you can go slowly to* (the place they are reluctant to visit) *and see what happens. Just take baby steps and communicate with me each step of the way.*

- *Stay calm and relaxed, become more and more relaxed with each breath. What are you doing now?*

- *Let me know when you are ready to* (go to the place) *and tell me what happens... It's very, very important for you to go back through this even though it's not pleasant. It'll free you to know. When you are ready, let me know.*

- (When they say "I don't think you want to know") *I want to help you. I think that your knowing about this will help you very, very much.*

- (When reporting that their recall is becoming unclear because of a fear) *Now I'm going to ask you to just relax. Breathe in golden light and for the next minute or so concentrate on breathing in golden light. I'm going to count again from 10 to 1. As I do your inner mind will double the relaxation. Just concentrate on breathing in golden light, beautiful, relaxing golden light and by the time we reach down to 1, you will be profoundly relaxed. You will be able to remember,*

116

experiencing freely. Meanwhile just relax deeper
and deeper... 10, 9, ...,5 just relaxing so deeply
with each count down... 4, 3, ..., 1, and now, tell
me more about this _____... What are you
doing?

Exploring Relationship Connections

The following questions can be used when a client is specifically interested in exploring relationships that span lives (and you may have used the partial script *A Relationship Connection* presented in the preceding chapter) or when you are doing a general Past Life exploration with the client. They are likely not appropriate when doing a Past Life Regression to address other specific client issues since they are not the focus of your inquiry.

- *Do you know (a person from the Past Life) in your current life? Could they be someone you know now, in another body?*

- *Come close, look into their eyes. People can change gender, the colour of their hair or skin, their whole look, but if you look into their eyes, you may recognize who the person is. Maybe it is someone you know from this life?*

- *Is there anyone in this lifetime who is with you now, as a different person?*

- *When you are looking into the eyes, do you have an instant recognition, as if you know this person from another life?*

- (To another life) *Is there any other life where you know this person? Take yourself to that life now. Take your time, there is no need to rush.*

When they answer "yes" to the above questions, give them some time to further identify the different roles those people play in their current or previous life. When they answer "no", you can move on. When they say, after a pause, "I'm not sure", you can give them a suggestion. *"That's alright. It may take some time for it to come to you. You will know it in a moment."* Then you move on. Very often they will tell you later on, typically after the death experience, because clients usually have a much wider perspective after being free from the constrains of a body. Or they may tell you after they come out of hypnosis, even if they are not one hundred percent certain. They may say something like, "I feel that person was my mother in this life. I'm not sure, but towards the end, I had this feeling."

Releasing Negative Energy

When you observe charged emotions and misconceptions during a Past Life Regression session, you can release them at the time, or at the end of a session, depending on the timing, intensity, and client's readiness. See also the section *Heal the Etheric Body* in Chapter 7.

If your client's Past Life personality has repressed anger, you can encourage the client to bring out the anger, and express it. For example if the anger is associated with someone who hurt them:

- *Tell the person how you feel about* (him/her).
  *Bring out all your emotions. Know that you can't
  be hurt anymore.*

A feeling of regret often comes with self-blame, and a
sense of guilt. The client needs to release those toxic feelings.
You can help them express those feelings and ask for
forgiveness, whether of themselves or from someone who is
present in the Past Life Regression. Note that within a Past
Life Regression, it is still possible to ask forgiveness of
someone who may already have died within the chronology
of the Past Life. For Example:

- *If you'd like, you can see* (him/her) *again. This
  person may not appear to be the one you were
  used to, but nevertheless, when* (he/she) *comes,
  there is no shadow of doubt that it is* (him/her).
  Tell (him/her) *now what you so wanted to say
  but had not had a chance to say before. Tell* (him/
  her) *everything you had not been able to express.*

- *Do you know there's another part to this? It's
  self-forgiveness. Say to yourself: I forgive you,*
  _____.

- *Is there anybody else you need to forgive in that
  lifetime?*

There are times that it may take more than once to
achieve forgiveness. A painful feeling can remain, though it
may be to a lesser degree. You can guide the client to go back
over the entire event again, and again, until the emotional

intensity is diminished and the story can be related with complete composure, and the emotion is neutralized.

If there is a physical pain from a past life that a client still feels in the current life - which may be the reason the client came to see you - you can guide the client to release it after you have reviewed the event.

- *All right, now that we've reviewed the story and you have learned from it, let's release the pain. You do not have to feel the pain in this body, in this life, or beyond. Let yourself be free now. For the next few breaths, with each exhale, let it go, more and more, with each exhale let it go. Take only the lessons, leave behind anything else.*

To release an emotion from the body, you need to first locate where it is in the body.

- *What are you feeling? ... What do you do with the* (specific feeling - e.g. despair)?

- *Can you identify a place in your body where the feeling is located?* (If so) *Where is it? Have you been carrying this* (specific feeling) *all the time in your* (the place in their body where the feeling is located)? *Do you think it's time to let go?*

- *It's not your fault. Somehow you know. You intuitively know. Visualize or imagine a bucket. Now you are going to drain the* (specific feeling) *out into the bucket... Now we are putting a lid on the bucket. Seal it. Let me know when it's sealed tight. Here comes some helium balloons, tied to the bucket, making it go up, all the way up, transformed into the sunlight. Let me know when it's completely transformed.*

You can also bring more light to the body part where the emotion was stored, to help them resolve the emotions.

- *Here comes a golden light, coming from your top of the head. As you breathe, breathe the energy around you.*

- *You feel safe here? While you feel safe here, I'm going to ask you a question: Does this lifetime as (past life personality) have any effect on* (client's name) *in the 21st century?*

- *Let's do a little something here. Tell* (past life name) *everything will be alright. Bring your 21st century self to him/her.*

Sometimes a client in a past life may have made a decision that would not serve them or even sabotage them, in this or another lifetime. For example they may have made a decision to "never trust again." When they have made these kinds of decisions, empower the client and help them undo the limiting beliefs as you would when treating a client outside of Past Life Regression.

You can also guide clients to discover their own realizations at the end of a Past Life Regression. The little epiphanies they can have at this time can also serve as an instant release of pent up emotions and energy.

- *3, 2, 1, ask your inner wisdom if there's anything else you need to know or learn today.*

- *I'll count from 3 to 1 one more time. On the count of 1, an insight comes to you. 3, 2, 1...*

As discussed in the previous sub-section, the moment of death can be a traumatic experience. The following script can help you release the energy when this is the case.

> *After all of your physical organs shut down, allow your soul to drift above your body. Just let me know when you're out and if you hear any other voices outside of you as the process is going on.*

> *The truth is that you're not dead. You are sitting in my office. If you can feel good re-experiencing your soul leave the body at death, you can surely feel this way while fully in your body. The anxiety, stress, and adrenaline you experienced prior to your death reinforced a survival script that has been letting you know you're still alive.*

When you resolve traumatic deaths, you can release negative energy associated with unconscious belief so that calm and peace will reinforce both survival and thriving.

> *If you can feel this freedom out of your body, you can feel it in the body. Allow yourself to be back in the body before the trauma. You know what*

happened to you. This experience is unfinished. Allow yourself to confront (the situation that led to their death). *Anger and sadness are normal emotions that need to be expressed.*

Sometimes releasing emotional energy is best achieved by allowing a client to physically act out the emotion. In this case you can use a pillow or cushion that the client can use for this purpose.

Do I have your permission to place a large pillow over your body?

(After the permission is given) *That's right, hit the pillow as you talk, and again, and again. Express your emotions. Take it all out. Very soon, you will feel much better. As you regain control of this situation, continue to speak everything that you're holding in your* (body part) *and throughout your body.*

If you perceive that the trauma in the Past Life may be affecting the client's current life or be related to their presenting issue(s) you may add the following statement.

This trauma may have negatively affected some aspects of your current life. Speaking of this trauma can help you unburden yourself both then and now.

Underneath your fear and anxiety may be other emotions. Allow yourself to go back into your body and express them. This can be an opportunity

to give voice to thoughts and emotions that were
withheld or unclear at the time. In other words,
allow yourself to hear your own voice and get to the
truth.

Advanced Techniques

The following two advanced techniques can be mind blowing for some people, though for some others they are natural and therefore normal. I have found them extremely enlightening and insightful. They are also quite easy to use, when you have suspended your disbelief that these may not be possible. You don't have to believe anything to test these techniques. Just test them, and see how it turns out.

Mind Merge

Mind merge is the ability to tap into others' thoughts and emotions. When we are in hypnosis, we all have this amazing ability, particularly relating to ourselves. It is like imagining yourself as another person and then feeling their thoughts and emotions about you. Mind merge is similar to what "Perceptual Position" is in Neuro-Linguistic Programming (NLP). It also has similarity to "Chair Therapy" in hypnotherapy.

Again and again I am amazed at how insightful this process can be for a client. One person can hold a grudge for someone else until the Mind Merge moment happens and then realize that person never meant to hurt, reject, or resent them.

This is a very powerful and therapeutic process and it can be very useful in Past Life Regression sessions.

A female client of mine was regressed to a Past Life where she was mute and deaf. When I was asking her questions, she attempted many times but could only produce some strange sounds. Eventually, the consciousness of my client came in and told me, "I don't think she can talk, she is mute and deaf." I had to ask the client to remain in the depth of trance, yet be able to observe what's going on and tell me the story as she observes it. Later, another key person appeared in the Past Life story – a boy that the mute girl liked very much. I instructed my client as the Past Life personality to become the boy, and tell me the rest of the Past Life story through him. My client was now doing a mind merge with this significant boy in her Past Life.

This was not only helpful, but also it was quite revealing for my client. By my client merging her mind with that of the boy and tapping into his thoughts and feelings about herself in that Past Life, many of her questions were automatically answered as her story was related to me by him.

As anther example, recall the story from the previous section, about a female client who was regressed to a life of a village boy, who lost his girlfriend to a rapid current. To allow self-forgiveness to take place, I used Mind Merge to have him become the spirit of the girl, who told me, it was actually her time to go, according to their pre-life agreement. By doing that, it gave the village boy a great chance to grow, to eventually become a leader.

A straightforward process for having a client enter and leave mind merge is as follows:

> *Now imagine stepping out of your body. Cross the space between you and* (the other person) *and step into* (his/her) *body. Come up into* (his/her) *head, turn and look out* (his/her) *eyes, merge with* (his/her) *mind and think* (his/her) *thoughts…* (*then you can learn where that person has learned that behaviour*, for example.)

Another way to do this is to ask the client to follow your instructions while you count from 3 to 1. As you count, quickly use your palm to cover their forehead and say, "*Become* (name of the other person)." Then tap on their forehead, and ask them questions directly as if they are that other person.

Afterwards, the client must be disconnected from the mind merge.

> (To the other) *We thank you, _____, for your assistance this day.*
>
> (To the client) *Separate and come out of* (his/her) *mind, step out of* (his/her) *body, come totally back into your own body and mind.*

126

Disconnect completely from (his/her) *energy.*
Come fully back into your own energy space.

Parallel Reality Regression

When a client is regressed to a Past Life, within one session, they can see the choices they have made in that life, and the consequences of those choices. At the end of the Past Life, you have the opportunity to help clients see if there were other alternative choices that they could have made, now that the whole Past Life is known to them, that they didn't notice in the moment they were reliving the events of that Past Life. A question I often ask is, *"Looking back, is there anything you could have done differently?"*

The end of a Past Life is a great opportunity for people to recognize options that they hadn't realized existed. Caught up in the unfolding of a life, people can feel trapped by a set of circumstances with few alternative courses of action. Acting based on those limited choices can leave them with an emotional burden for the rest of that life and beyond.

Sometimes for clients simply acknowledging that they had other options is enough to release any emotional burden. However other times they may need to experience the difference which those other options could have made. That means that they need to "live" an alternative choice, decision or action to the full term in order to fully understand the consequences of that choice. By doing so, the burden of being trapped is replaced by an expanded awareness of their own innate power which was previously unrecognized.

A client of mine carried a lot of guilt and shame with her. She'd been dealing with self-doubt and unworthiness for a while. When she came to see me for Past Life Regression, during one of her sessions, she went to a Past Life where she was a knight named Harold. During an argument with his stepfather, who had always treated him abusively and arrogantly, Harold became out of control and viciously sliced his father to death. Looking at his father's lifeless body, he instantly felt horrible, shame and guilt. He couldn't believe what he had done even though he didn't think he had a choice the moment he did it.

He carried those emotions with him to the end of his life and over to another life.

I decided to guide Harold back to the moment of the argument again. The argument is going on. Harold is extremely angry and almost out of control. His hand goes to the sword, and he pulls it out. However, this time, I ask him to pause, and ask him, "Knowing that you will probably regret and feel horrible, is this what you really want to do?"

"I hate him so much."

"Yes. You hate him so much. Yet instead of slicing him, do you have other options?"

Eventually Harold decided to walk away, and he never saw his stepfather again in that lifetime. Consequently he never had to carry the guilt and shame over his father's murder. This in turn was a lens through which my client could evaluate the need of her own sense of guilt and shame.

The realization that one has better choices is very powerful. More of Harold's story can be found at: *https:// kemilahypnosis.com/past-lives/regression-into-a-probable-past-lifetime-nora/*. You can also read other parallel reality regression stories at: *https://kemilahypnosis.com/category/ parallel-lives/*.

In another client's past life, in the United States during the 19th century, out of desperation, the woman jumped into a well and committed suicide. After death, with the help of a spirit guide, she realized that she could have had another choice. We tapped into that parallel reality and she saw how things worked out. She eventually moved to France and lived a full life in that parallel reality. This felt to her just as real as the suicidal Past Life that she had initially regressed to, but it showed her that she did have choices and did have power over life situations. Read more of this client casework at: *https:// kemilahypnosis.com/past-lives/what-we-learn-from-a-past-life-suicide/*.

In one of my presentations, a hypnotherapist asked me if doing Parallel Reality Regression is to plant a false memory. My short answer was that if it's for the purpose of healing, forgiveness and self-empowerment, I don't mind clients engaging in such *what-if* scenarios.

If it's for the purpose of blaming, self-victimization and accusation, I have no business doing it.

As a hypnotherapist, I don't really know where their Past Life memories come from in the first place. Could not their "original" Past Life memory be just one probable reality? Looking at the bigger picture, since time doesn't really exist, maybe a truer name for Past Life Regression could be Probable Reality Examination.

When you undertake Parallel Reality Regressions with clients, you are doing so with their knowledge and understanding. Recall that it starts with your question to them about whether they could have done things differently. When they undertake Parallel Reality Regression they are aware that they are engaged in a thought experiment to help them understand that they often have choices in life that may not be obvious when caught up in the details of a situation.

We don't really know how memories work. Everything is perception. The past doesn't exist anywhere but in our perception. We do actually create memories of the "past" in the present, as the present is the only moment that there is. If a person has problems in their life, it may be because they already carry with them false memories.

Parallel Reality Regression allows clients to explore possibilities in the context of a Past Life. So the long answer to that question is: If it is self-empowerment to the client, if it gives them the power to make the decisions they need to make in their life, to know that they are in control of their reality – then Parallel Reality Regression is a genuine experience that can be of benefit to them.

CHAPTER 7

After Death

After death can be the end of a Past Life Regression for some clients and hypnotherapists. But when clients are open to exploring beyond death, I personally prefer to go further, as some types of healing require death to be just the beginning. Interlife Regression (also called "Life Between Lives Regression") is itself a fascinating modality beyond the pieces we touch upon in this chapter.

First you will transition the client to the non-physical. Then you will guide the client to move beyond earthly existence, and further assist them with physical and emotional healing. Finally, you will bring them to both a life review and a karma review. Beyond that, you can bring the client to a Life Planning stage, or the pre-birth planning for the current life.

Transitioning

This can be a moment of confusion when people may potentially experience a wide variety of things. Sometimes a client can instantly know what's going on and volunteer information; but most of the time, a client may simply wait

133

there for further instructions. Try not to lead a client on what they should experience as everyone may experience or interpret the afterlife differently, based on their cultural or religious background, personal development, and belief system. However, depending on your judgement of the situation, sometimes it may help to give them some general guidance, such as *"Begin to move upward, feeling light and free, experiencing an elation. Maybe a bright light appears in the distance…"* If this is not the client's experience, they will simply correct you, and then you can follow their lead.

Many people experience an inter-dimensional shift which is normally interpreted as a tunnel of light. People coming back from a near death experience (NDE) often describe, "As I look up, there was a tunnel - a light, an opening. I move towards it, but my feet don't touch a floor. "

Some eager souls may simply jump right into another lifetime after death. When this happens, I find the clients normally have hundreds, if not thousands, of lifetimes. They seem to be attached to earth lives, or simply eager to make spiritual growth. Or, maybe the afterlife realm doesn't exist in their conscious understanding or their cultural background so they skip it entirely.

Below are some of the scripts you can choose to use for guiding a client into the afterlife experience.

Beginning and Reflection

Now connect to that last breath of that life.
Get out of your body now. Before you transcend to
that soul plane, as you start floating free from the

body. I want you to stay there for a moment, hovering over that body. Look down at the physical body of that life. Describe what you are seeing there. How many people are there around your body?

Can you identify those people there? Just look at them. In this soul state, is there an instant recognition?

Move a little bit further away from the physical. Is there anyone you need to say goodbye to?

Can you look into their eyes, and see if you know these people today, in this life?

(Going to their own funeral) *Would you like to go to your own funeral?* (If the answer is yes) *3..., 2..., and 1. Be there now. Describe what you see. As a guest of honour, is there anyone there noticing you?*

When the Life Was Fearful

You don't need anxiety, pain, and fear to know you're alive. These feelings have been part of your survival-script dictating that pain and suffering, although unpleasant, were necessary because they were the last feelings present before death. This script can end as you become conscious of it and resolve the past. Your intuition will expand and you will know whom you can trust. And as you move out of the role of victim you will become a benign observer, someone no longer motivated by those negative emotions.

Moving Beyond Earthly Existence

Now, you may or may not be greeted by friends or relatives immediately. This is a personal matter, as always. Overall, you may be more interested in people that you have known in past lives than those close to you in the present one, for example. What comes to your awareness now?

Telepathy can operate without distortion in this period. And your own motives will be crystal clear.

Examine the fabric of the existence you have left. Learn to understand how your experiences were the result of your own thoughts and emotions and how these affected others. After this examination is through, you will be aware of the larger portions of your own identity.

When you realize the significance and meaning of the life you have just left, then you are ready for conscious knowledge of your other existences.

So become aware of an expanded awareness. Tell me what happens next?

And now I'd like you to move forward in time to the next significant event. Staying in the

spirit state... 3, 2, 1... what are you aware of?
Where are you now and what are you experiencing?

Heal the Etheric Body

The death and after death moment can be an excellent chance to release physical pains, illness, and burdens, especially those related to issues that were shared during the client intake. Clearing energetic imprints from the etheric body prevents them from being carried from one lifetime to another. See also Releasing Negative Energy in the previous chapter which focuses more on negative emotions and misconceptions that you notice during the Past Life experience.

Below are some questions and instructions that you may find useful in guiding clients at this stage.

- *Now, I want you to check out any areas of your body as to where you are holding these* (pains, illness, or burdens). *As you have done with this life as* _____, *how would you like it to be released?*

- (If the body is torn open) *as you rise towards the light, fill the torn spaces in the etheric body with light. Imagine light coming in from the brightness above you. Funnel light into every space in your etheric form. Let your etheric body be fully healed. Can you see the light coming in? ... How does it feel?... Is it full yet?.... How does that feel?*

137

- (Healing loss) *Now move a little further away… How does your spirit evaluate what you have done? Do you find your* (whatever is lost) *in that dimension?*

- (If after death the body couldn't move on) *Imagine the body being taken to the spirit realm and cleansed in a healing waterfall of energy.*

- (After a life filled with chronic adverse circumstances) *From the retrospective, what moments of choice did you have?*

- (Soul Purifying) *Gently move through a translucent screen. Pull out all the negative things that you had accumulated in your experiences in that lifetime, so you will leave behind those things in that lifetime where they belong.*

- *And you will only move to the "Other Side" taking the positive and leaving behind all negative.*

Life Review

After death, many people encounter "Beings of Light", "Beings dressed in white", or similar. There is also the possibility that people may be reunited with deceased loved ones. All of these beings may help them do a life review. A Life Review is a purposeful and contemplative examination of a life, in contrast to the experience of "seeing one's life flash before one's eyes" that is common at the realization that death is imminent.

This is the moment that clients may receive knowledge about their life and the nature of the universe.

In this moment, I want you to progress ahead, to a time when you are in higher spiritual realms. There you are, in contact with your guides, and beings of light, in contact with the source. In this soul state, you can instantly connect to the higher realms…

5…you can be there instantly, where you can make review of the life with the help of your guides.

4… 3… 2… and 1… I want you to be there. And just make a review. Let all the significant memories of that life once again flash to you. From this place of higher dimension, you can start narrating to me about that life.

After guiding them to the Life Review stage, below are some questions that you may find useful to ask your client.

- *What lessons have you learned from that life? In this higher spiritual state of consciousness, you can understand the essence of that past life.*

- *What are you experiencing at this point of time? Describe it more. How are you feeling there?*

- *Good. As a soul, do you have any form? Just notice, describe yourself.*

- *What are you doing now? From this broader perspective, what is the purpose in experiencing that lifetime?*

- *If there's anything that prevented you from changing your life, what is it?*

If your client has expressed that they would have liked to have lived the life differently but are unable to articulate how that could have come about, you may want to consider *Parallel Reality Regression*, as discussed in the previous chapter, either in this or a subsequent session.

- *What connection was there between* _____ (presenting problem) *and that lifetime?*

- *Looking back, is there any unfinished business in this life as* _____ _____ (the Past Life personality name)? *If you had a second chance, how differently would you do or be in that life?*

- *Could you be carrying something of that man/woman in you today?*

- *Will you contact your higher self now, and see what you can do to forgive yourself, and leave this experience in the past where it belongs?*

- *Get an intuitive understanding as for the nature of your whole self. See how it has placed you in a position in which certain abilities, insights, and experiences can be realized, and in which your unique kind of consciousness can be nurtured.*

- *You've punished yourself enough… would you be willing to release this need to punish yourself?*

As mentioned above, spirit guides or archangels may be present when doing the past life review. When the clients hesitate in answering some of those questions, you can make it easier by asking them to ask their guides. Many times, a client will spontaneously give their voice to a guide or an angel, who comes through and speaks directly to you. This is a moment when great insights can be found. I have even received personal and professional information through the channeled messages from Archangels. Dr. Brian Weiss mentioned similar things in his bestselling book, *Many Lives, Many Masters.*

When you see fit, you don't have to wait until a guide spontaneously speaks through your client. You can evoke the voice of a guide by asking your client to trust and allow the voice of a guide to come through. Speak to your client first, *"You can give your guide a voice. This guide is now with you, helping you for the life review. And you do trust him/her, don't you? Allow the guide to come through and speak if you may, so that I will have a direct communication with him/her. (Calling the guide's name if it was identified), please come through when you are ready. And when you are here, simply say the words, 'I'm here.'"* Then you can wait until a slightly different tone or voice says, "I'm here." If a guide's voice doesn't come through, usually it's fear in the client that blocks it. In that case, you can simply continue to have your client communicate between you and the guide.

Karma Review

Karma is the law of moral causation. Basically it is about energy balance and imbalance. Whenever there is an imbalance, the soul wants to bring it back in balance. That's how nature works.

Karma is not meant to be judgemental, at least in therapy sessions. Western religions may use the concepts of "heaven" and "hell" to motivate the behaviour of living people through reward and punishment. And sometimes "Karma" may have a similar connotation in people. However these definitions are not how we use the term here. Part of a Karmic Review is freeing people from a narrow focus of reward and punishment to a broader perspective of overall balance. All Karmic imbalance is ultimately self-imposed for some reason. To balance the imbalance is to receive whatever lesson was its intrinsic purpose and move on.

Karma Review also allows clients to connect different lifetimes. Below are examples of questions that you may find useful during a Karma Review. Come up with your own questions as appropriate to your clients' situations.

- *What emotions and feelings do you carry from the lifetime as you separate from the body?* (If time allows) *Let that* (feeling or sensation) *take you right back into another lifetime. Locate another life that you felt that way.*

- (If the body was killed) *In this calm state, allow the mind to be crystal clear. Sometime we switch roles in different lifetimes. Connect with other lifetimes; see if you have met the soul of* (the killer) *before, in another lifetime maybe?*

- *Is there anything you need to say or do to the people you left?*

- *Move a little bit further away... Is there anyone you need to forgive?*

- *Now let's move forward. Release anything you don't need from the past so that you can move unburdened into the future. Release any unbalanced karmic energy. Let it go.*

- *Is there another lifetime involved with the events in the lifetime you have just explored?* (Pause for answer) *Locate that lifetime.*

- *Locate the event in that other lifetime that set the forces in motion that led to the situation in the lifetime just explored.*

- *Locate the Karmic event that led to the present-life conflict.*

- *Now, make any connection between that life and this. Draw any parallels with this current life, any particularly active resonance. What does that life have to do with your present one?*

- *How does this story relate to your current life?*

Pre-Life Planning Stage

No matter which time era a Past Life Regression reveals, after death, you can easily bring a client to the Pre-Life or Pre-Birth Planning stage of this life. The soul's experience and perception can be very enlightening to the client's mind-body personality.

One client came in for a Past Life Regression session telling me how alienated she felt from her parents. Her mother gave birth to her as a teenager. The parents were divorced when she was a young girl. She grew up mostly with her grandmother. She always felt neglected by both of her parents, well into adulthood. There was significant resentment in her tone when she talked about her parents.

She had a Past Life as a young Scottish soldier who died during the second world war, his dreams of returning to his village, marrying, and writing a book unfulfilled. After death, I brought the spirit to the Life Planning stage for her current life.

We reviewed the choices she had for different families, geographic locations, and genders. That was when she told me she chose her parents. She described how eager she was to experience this life. She had to plan carefully for the pregnancy of her young mother. "It was challenging to plan for that, as they didn't live together, but I made it!" There was a victorious smile on the corners of my client's lips.

That smile was the opposite to the tone of victim she had when she presented herself as an "unwanted baby" and I even started to feel sorry for her parents. Asked further for any agreement between her parents and her, she said, "Of course there is an agreement, as it always is."

Through this revelation, she now doesn't feel uncared for by her parents. She understands now that she chose her parents, on a much deeper level, purposefully not to have much connection so she could be independent at an early age, and then start to write her books, the books that Scottish soldier never had a chance write.

You can start a regression to the Pre-Life Planning Stage by simply instructing the client as follows:

Now on the count of three, move towards the Life Planning stage. It's where you plan for the current life. Allow any guides or spiritual helpers to help you there. 1, 2, 3, be there now. What comes to your awareness?

Often people can't fathom whether the "place" they find themselves is inside or outside. Mostly it's "both inside and outside". If they pause too long without answering, you can say, "It may be hard to make out where you are. Maybe you are somewhere that you feel both inside and outside at the same time. Just notice what is immediately in front of you."

The answer that you will receive will often be along the lines of a table, a ring, a screen, a big book with moving pictures, a crystal ball… Regardless of the specific answer you get, you can guide your client during this process. The following questions will help you elicit meaningful information:

- *Are you aware of any other higher beings here? Or are you in this place of life selection alone?*

- *Have you selected your upcoming life yet?*

- *How many options are offered to you for the next life? Besides the one you've chosen, tell me the others. What kind of family? Country? Profession? Gender? Why did you reject them?*

- *What made you select this life as* (the client's name)? *What kind of specific challenges are there? What kind of goals can living this life this way help you achieve?*

Your client may be offered only one of two body choices, or they may be given up to five. The life choices for those bodies could be defined as easy, more challenged, or arduous. The reasons for the number and types of choices depends on motivational desires, karmic issues, and evolutionary age.

The client seems to always have a sense of control over what they see, with earthly devices such as dials, knobs, buttons, or touch screens. After viewing their body choices, you can guide clients to view snapshots of events from their current life, either previous to the present time, or a most likely future in a matrix of probabilities, or both. It depends on the purpose of the work you are doing with each client. Snapshots of the past are like Age Regression. Snapshots of the future are like Age Progression.

You can also ask the clients about their relationships. End the session by connecting their life with their life purpose. After all, many clients may come to see you for clarification of that, and those who don't come for that, often find that information to be a fruitful conclusion to their session.

- *Do you see certain people in the snapshots you are supposed to work with in this life?*

- *Overall, that is the purpose of living this life? Are you living your life according to what you are viewing here? If not what is the difference? And why?*

- *Is there anything else that you see in the snapshots that we have not discussed? Would you like to?*

CHAPTER 8

Post Regression Contextualization and Exit

At the end of a Past Life Regression session, you need to utilize your insights to contextualize the learning, and give relevant suggestions, directly and indirectly to the client. This is the moment to combine intake notes, the presenting issues, and what occurred during the Past Life Regression, to give clients specific suggestions, so that the learning can be further anchored in their awareness, consciously and unconsciously.

After providing specific suggestions, in many cases it is also beneficial to give general suggestions, such as the following:

> *Draw all your attention to the sound of my voice. This reminds you that you are the most important person in your life. You want the best, not to settle for less. You walk with your strength, with pride. You project peacefulness and wisdom to the world. Others notice the change in you of strength and graciousness. This is the gift that's*

given to you from _____ (name of the person they were in the Past Life).

Your past is your assets; your future is your strength. You're no longer affected by the past.

As you awake, you will begin to gain more insight from your universal inner wisdom, your higher self, and information from your past lives. More and more memories will continue to reveal themselves. Now you have your higher self to guide you. Some of the memories will continue to flood into your awareness, in your dreams while you sleep, or in the silent moments of your life. When you awaken, you will know what you know. You will be physically relaxed, mentally clear, emotionally calm, and spiritually awake.

0... Let's close that subconscious door. Everything becomes neutralized at this number. Come back to your normal awareness. Take only the wisdom, leaving behind the negativity.

1... Realize the oneness of your mind and body, heart and soul, conscious and subconscious; all come into one harmoniously for your highest good.

2... Slowly, calmly, easily coming back to this time and space.

3... Feel the new energy come to your body. From the top of the head to the tips of the toes, feeling wonderful in every way.

4... is a nicely alert number, becoming aware of the chair beneath you, and the room around you.

5... eyes open, wide awake, fully alert, and notice how good you feel after knowing the depth of who you are.

CHAPTER 9

Afterward

One day in January 2014, a 20-year-old young woman contacted me for anxiety that she had been feeling, especially in social situations. She had recently come to study in Vancouver from California. Feeling alone, and uncertain with almost everything in her life, she needed help. Her father, who she didn't grow up with, found me online and sent my information to her.

Amy (not her real name) is tall and very beautiful. I was a little bit taken aback by the light in her eyes. She has this greenish eye colour, very bright and sparkly. She did not tell me whether she particularly believed in reincarnation or not. But I have noticed that young people I see these days are often spiritually open, so I said to her, on our second appointment, "We may need to go all the way to the cause of this anxiety. It can be as far as we need to go. Do you understand?"

She nodded her head.

Then I asked, "Before Amy, who were you? Have you ever thought about it? 21 years ago, where were you?"

"Another existence." After thinking for a while, she said, "I suppose".

We did not plan to do a Past Life Regression. We objectified the anxiety in her chest and throat area and asked it to take us to its cause. Amy's inner mind took us to a teenage male's life where he was extremely shy and fearful about his overpowering, much older brother. That brother turned out to be Amy's mother in this life. The boy's mother was protective but powerless in front of his brother. His brother eventually managed to send the mother away. We also discovered that the mother was Amy's father in this life, who was "sent away" through divorce when Amy was 2.

The spontaneous Past Life Regression seemed to make sense to Amy on a deeper level and I didn't need to explain much to her. Amy continued to see me for the following five months for social and relationship issues. In one of our last sessions, Amy spontaneously went to a "castle" with clouds inside, and there she met her spirit guide, who introduced himself as Julius Caesar. He told her this life is all about "spiritual awakening" – a term that Amy, busy with her school and on-again-off-again boyfriend relationship, was not familiar with. Her guide told her that seeking hypnotherapy was a way to have me, the catalyst, trigger the awakening. Her guide also confirmed my role in her life, and confirmed that Amy and I had met each other before in another life, both as warriors. (More of Amy's and my story can be found at this link: *https://kemilahypnosis.com/ past-lives/awakening-warrior-within/*.)

During the session, Amy was very resistant to the idea of Julius Caesar as her guide because he is too famous. She said she made it up.

I have met this kind of resistance before. Occasionally a client of mine would be regressed to a past life being someone who is well-known. Very rarely would my clients easily embrace it. Instead they tend to dismiss the regression information saying they have made it up, or read too many historic books. In Amy's case, having Julius Caesar as her guide was too much to be true.

Once I heard another Past Life Regressionist say that some people are ego-driving. They want to see if they were famous in a Past Life. "Not so many people could be Cleopatra in a Past Life, you know." That Past Life Regressionist may have a point. But even famous people reincarnate too, don't they?

In my work I have found people to be quite the opposite from what that Regressionist claimed. Maybe that's just the kind of people I attract. But my experience is that clients readily accept having been a farmer, a housewife, a teacher, or any ordinary existence, and they have a hard time when they happen to have been someone that anyone would know. They would tell me what's going on in regression but constantly judge, even in trance, "This can't be true. I must be making it all up."

One way I address this is that I have them imagine their best friend and bring their face in front of them. Then I ask them to see if they can change their friend's hairstyle, maybe add or remove glasses on their face, or change their outfit. Normally they can easily do that. I then tell them, "You just made it up. The glasses and hairstyle."

I then tell them, while still in hypnosis, that when things don't feel right, that they can't just make up any information. In Amy's case, I told her, after re-emerging her, "You've tried to deny it, but the being you saw in the castle insisted on calling himself Julius Caesar, no matter how much you wanted him to change his name. You tried hard to change his heavy costume, dressed as a gladiator, but you didn't succeed. You didn't because you were not making it up. If you made it up, you could have easily changed and manipulated those things, just as you did with your best friend."

Amy's eyes became even brighter on that note. **"It feels good to trust one's unconscious mind"** was all I could think of when I saw the sparks in her eyes.

Seeing her eyes lighten up, I knew from every cell in my being, why, without choice, I have chosen to do what I do in this lifetime.

Acknowledgements

My deepest gratitude goes to Tim Melanchuk, my remarkable editor, art designer, friend, and life partner. Tim is an engineer, and Past Life Regression truly doesn't do too much to him. Yet his unconditional love and support towards whatever I fall into is so extraordinary that I feel I will have several more lifetimes to pay him back, happily, eagerly and lovingly. Thank you Tim. On that Canada Day meeting you at the Jazz Festival in David Lam Park, little did I imagine what delicious life could unfold for me. You have witnessed all the years, all the tears, fears, frustrations, laughter, excitements and celebrations on my becoming what I was meant to be, even before I was born.

I am indebted to all of the people who gave me their deepest trust and had me conduct Past Life Regressions with them. It was sacred moments for them. And I hold those moments with all my heart. You all have been my best teachers. I am very grateful to some of you who have given me permission to write your marvellous stories in this book and in my blog. (For my Past Life Regression clients case stories, visit: *https://kemilahypnosis.com/category/past-lives/*.) It is so enlightening to know I have met with some of you before in other lifetimes. What a small world!

For her trust and unbeatable clarity on thinking, my appreciation goes to my colleague and ARCH (Association of Registered Clinical Hypnotherapists) president Heather Flanagan. She doesn't know it, but this book wouldn't be a manifestation, at least not the way it is manifested, without her.

I am very grateful to my instructors and mentors Dr. Brick Saunderson and Mona Saunderson, who generously held my hands into the wonder of hypnotherapy, and who continue to encourage and support me and many others.

Special thanks to my colleagues Cori Jackson, Sylvain Joseph, Gerda Toffoli and Alma Pasic, whose friendship I enjoy very much. You all have helped me in one way or another shape the pages of this book.

References

Bhulman, William (2000). Exploring Your Past Lives. Audio CDs.

Weiss, Brian (1988), Many Lives, Many Masters. Reed Business Information, Inc.

Newton, Kondaveti, M.D. Life Research Academy.

Webster, Richard (2001). Practical Guide to Past-Life Memories: Twelve Proven Methods. Llewellyn Publications.

Newton, Michael, Ph.D (2010). Life Between Lives, Hypnotherapy for Spiritual Regression. Llewellyn Publications.

Have a "client intake form"
The Interview -
    client Background
    Reason for being here.
    History with [illegible]

    Why? - 3 reasons
        client asks
        helpful for some proce
        sp of [illegible] cou

    intake →